NOW PURPOSE MANUAL

HOW TO FIND YOUR LIFE'S CALLING TODAY

S. Ali Myers

ISBN-13: 978-1974588169
ISBN-10: 1974588165

DEDICATION

This book is dedicated to my children Kalil, Nas, and Tahj. I love you unconditionally and am looking forward to seeing you live your purpose.

ACKNOWLEDGEMENTS

This book is about purpose. There are many souls who helped me get to where I'm at today so I can live my purpose. I'm eternally grateful to everyone who played a part in my life, big or small. Every lesson, challenge, blessing, and reward I have ever received, molded me into the being I am today.

In no particular order.

I believe we all choose our parents before coming to earth. Looking back now, I know why I chose mine. Thank you to my mother, Karen Elaine Pipkin, for allowing me to explore reality on my own terms and always accepting who I am. You have never tried to make me be something I'm not. I will always honor you. Thank you to my biological father for teaching me how to be a man. Even though you weren't in my life, you taught me a valuable lesson of making sure I'm present in my children's lives. For that, I sincerely appreciate you.

There is one person who has been consistently by my side in my adult years, through thick and thin, providing unconditional love and support. Sanserae, I appreciate you more than I let on. We have traveled through lifetimes together forever. Thank you for being the catalyst that has helped me help so many people help themselves. You have always been my biggest supporter. I don't know where I would be right now if it not for you.

Honors and praises to my most influential teachers, Masters, Dr. Mitchell Gibson and Bro. Panic. Completely different in their approach but with more overlapping ideologies than you can detect with the naked ear. Father (Gibson), you have demonstrated what mastery looks like on so many levels. Not only have you set the bar, you have shown me spiritually how to reach it. I absolutely adore you and Mother Acharya with all my heart and appreciate you both beyond words. My brother, Pan, you are a legend. You taught me that I can be myself and still have a high degree of mastery and spiritual maturity. There is no one on the planet as real in the spiritual game as you are. Thank you for showing me the way.

I use the phrase "ambassador of your family" to describe the black sheep. The black sheep is the one person in the family who takes a more spiritual or metaphysical approach. Even though I use that term, I can honestly say beyond a shadow of a thought, that I'm not the black sheep of my family. I was blessed to incarnate into a family with blood cousins who are all conscious and awake on one level or another. Special shouts out to my cousins who are more like brothers, Jason, Juice and Orlando. And, my girl cousins, April, Janae and the twins, Tia and Tiara. Juice, you have been down since day one. Still to this day one of the coolest cats on the planet. Taught me how to be myself. It's an honor to share blood with you and I'm looking forward to reading your first book. O, even though we've had our ups and downs throughout life, you know I love you more than anything. When I felt like there was no one out there that cared about what I had to share, you were there encouraging me to shine my light. You and Juice played a huge role in me being able to teach publicly. Janae, even though we didn't grow up super tight, it's like you're my little sister as well as one of the realest chicks out there! Jason, you are the youngest male cousin but, probably the most powerful. Your humility, discipline, dedication and commitment are off the charts. It's humbling to know you're my family.

To my little sister, Kelina. You know bubby loves you. You are absolutely one of the sweetest souls on the planet. Humanity can learn so much from you. Continue to stay pure and adorable.

I've been blessed to have non-relatives be my family. Spiritual family to be more specific. I believe that your spiritual family may be more important than your biological one when you're on the path to enlightenment. There are many souls I consider my Fam but there are a few who I share a close bond with. Much love, peace, and gratitude to Jeremy Trent (peace and blessings be upon you), Rob G., Rob Cole, Corey Smith, Maurice aka Mo Squared, Sy Shanti, Mill, Chris Enlightened and his wife, Nykky. I appreciate the relationship I have with each of you. Chris and Mo, I especially appreciate your trust and faith in our bond. I honestly know you are there for me if I need anything and vice versa. Chris, like I've told you before, I appreciate you more than you know.

Now Purpose Manual would not have been completed to my standards (edited and proofread) if it weren't for two souls, Dee Majewski and Janell A. Morgan. The Universe sent you to me and you both delivered! Janell, I am humbled and grateful for you going way beyond what I asked for and making this book as good as I feel it is.

To my Myers and Stone family, I have nothing but love for you. Grandma Donna Jean and Uncle Buster (peace and blessings be upon you), I love you. Special recognition to some family members who helped me in my growth. To my uncles, William (Billy) and Aahmes. Uncle Billy, I am eternally grateful to you and your wife, Aunt Ellen, for helping to raise me and caring for me as one of your own. I will never forget you being the first, and only adults to take me on vacation as a child. Those memories are etched in eternity. Uncle Aahmes, I remember you coming and playing with me and teaching me life lessons. You were always mature but so child-like. I remember more than you probably know about how you were with me. You taught and did things you didn't have to. I'm grateful. Aunt Kim and Aunt Kathy, I love you both so much. Aunt Kathy, I will always cherish our conversations when O was at work. You really are the best aunt one can ask for. And, Aunt Kim, mom still to this day tells me about how crazy you were about me. I adore you and you know I will take you anywhere lol.

Peace and blessings be upon my grandmother and grandfather, William and Norma Myers. Grandma, you were and still are my greatest teacher. You more than prepared me for this world.

To everyone who has inspired me, thank you.

To all my students, clients and fans. I love you.

TABLE OF CONTENTS

INTRODUCTION

Have you ever asked yourself the question, "What is my purpose?"

Trust that you are not alone. Throughout the vast expanse of history, man has pondered his or her existence. It can be surmised that man has always had an innate knowing that life has a deeper meaning.

To date, there is a great deal of content available to help one discover their life's purpose. This book, *Now Purpose Manual*, is not the only text to help you discover your purpose, and I'm definitely not the only person who teaches about the subject. To be honest, there is no *one* particular way to discover who you are and what your purpose is. The only *right* way is the way that helps you the most.

It is my desire that *Now Purpose Manual* offers clarity and insight into what is possible for you in life. The language in this book is programmed to have you focus on the now. The present moment is the most precious time we have. This is why the present is a gift. Are you choosing to open it and use it, or do you discard it, treating it like an ugly pair of socks?

The term, *Now Purpose*, is defined as what you can do today. Not tomorrow or next year. *Today*. Actually, you probably could've done it yesterday. The point is, you have all that you need to fulfill your purpose right now even though you may not feel like you are where you want to be. What you do today will take you to where you will be tomorrow. Just because your ideal vision of life seems far off, it doesn't mean you don't have what you need today to get there. It only seems far away because you haven't put in enough effort to reach it. Do your best to avoid viewing your life's purpose and calling as something that is in the future. Even if you have a clear idea of what you want to do, it doesn't matter if you're not doing it. The trick is to condition yourself to do the things now that will get you closer to your vision. Again, *Now Purpose*. What can you do *today*?

Our society has conditioned us to think that achievement and success come overnight. There are many so-called celebrities, in the mainstream and social media, who portray themselves as being bigger than what they are. The combination of unrealistic expectations and lack of patience is a killer on the path to more purpose. Comparing your life to someone else's is another whammy that deters one from reaching their purpose. Many souls are suffering from jealousy and envy thanks to social and mainstream media sources. Your environment and family can produce jealousy too. If you are comparing yourself to others, you may even be affected by envious thoughts on a subconscious level. What someone else does is their business. If you find yourself feeling envious, jealous or uncomfortable in any way, it's likely because you're paying too much attention to them. Wouldn't that energy be better used if it were focused on what *you* can do? Wouldn't you be more fulfilled witnessing the unfolding of your own growth as opposed to watching someone else shine?

2

Now Purpose Manual will be helpful in the process of reframing your focus. The chapters of this book are written to re-train your mind to be more oriented to concentrate on your individual purpose and passion so that you can begin to feel more fulfilled and live a life that is more satisfying. With chapters like *How to Live Your Now Purpose* and *8 Keys to Living Your Now Purpose*, you will discover the areas of life that resonate most powerfully for you while learning ways to place focus on what you are able to control rather than being distracted by your ego's tendency to make up reasons why you are not where you're supposed to be based on unhealthy comparison. Concepts such as these are the ideal starting point for finding your purpose.

As cliché as it may sound, life is what you make it. As individuals with varying interests, we are each naturally drawn to different facets of reality. Some people find their bliss by centering their lives on their family. Others may find fulfillment in their careers. Creative people think life is about expressing themselves. Entertainers may think life is about having fun. The point is your reality is what you make it. Regardless of any external circumstance, you will identify with whatever resonates with you. What you resonate with most directly relates to your life's purpose. This internal knowing cannot be validated by anyone, only confirmed or suggested. You know what you should be doing. Your heart is the best judge.

Knowing that you are in control of your life will greatly increase your chances of being purposeful. Knowing which area of life to prioritize will almost guarantee your success. Disallowing others to dictate what is important to you will assist you in finding your true path. You can be open to suggestions and feedback, but avoid placing too much pressure on others. Your purpose is about *you* and what *you* can do for yourself and others. Master self and others will assist you.

The *Now Purpose Manual* was written for anyone seeking greater happiness in life. When we do things we find purpose in, we automatically raise our vibration. This vibration translates to joy, fulfillment, accomplishment, confidence and other positive emotions. This book will help you clearly see what is right in front of you. Many times, friends, family and loved ones see our greatness and potential before we do. Other times, those we trust don't seem to have faith in us. Both scenarios are reminders to stay self-sustained and self-motivated. Only what YOU believe becomes true. The more energy you put into what is in your heart to do, the more confident you will become. Confidence is reinforced by doing the "right" thing. The "right" thing is your *Now Purpose* – what you should be doing *today*.

You will find the bulk of your *Now Purpose* in what is called the Lights of Awareness™. The Lights of Awareness are things we *feel* like we should be doing, but are not doing. They are the thoughts that keep replaying in our minds to do something or not do something. As you uncover your Lights, you will find your Now

Purpose. The Lights are literally the action steps to get to your goal.

Now Purpose Manual was delivered to my consciousness based on the Lights of Awareness. As a Spiritual Teacher, many have asked me how to find their life's purpose. The answer I was spiritually given lies in the Lights of Awareness. The Lights should be your focus right now. This makes them extremely purposeful.

I hope you're ready to take a deep dive into yourself! I assure you, if you follow the suggestions in this book, you will find yourself feeling more fulfilled and living with deeper passion and purpose.

How to Use This Book

Before you start reading this book, I want you to know that this process is all about YOU. Nothing I say in this book should trump what you feel in your heart and soul. However, I would like to share with you the way that I would recommend you use the *Now Purpose Manual*.

Make certain to read the chapter, *8 Keys to Living Your Now Purpose*. It will provide a solid foundation for what this book is about. Most of the questions that you may have while figuring out your *Now Purpose* are probably addressed within the 8 keys.

Next, read the chapter, *Lights of Awareness*. Understanding and being conscious of your Lights is what makes *Now Purpose* work. Your Lights are the activities that guide your life. It would be extremely beneficial for you to become more aware of them.

The Lights of Awareness may be enough to get you started on your path, but if you still have doubts, choose the area of life you are drawn to and go to that chapter. Each area of life chapter is designed to guide you to your purpose in that area. These chapters provide optimal starting points for you to begin living your *Now Purpose*.

Now Purpose Manual can also be used as a workbook of sorts. In each area of life chapter, there is an activity along with awareness questions for you to complete and examples for you to review specific to each area of life. Take your time and be honest and action-oriented in your answers.

Now Purpose Manual also contains chapters for universal purposes and guidance. We all share common life purposes and receive spiritual guidance which is outlined in the respected chapters. Once you know your purpose for today, allow the guidance to direct you and be cognizant of general purposes that everyone shares. This will help you recognize all of the opportunities available to you and be able to take advantage of them.

The book ends with a Q & A chapter. If you still have concerns after reading *Now Purpose Manual*, make sure to review the commonly asked questions. More than likely, your concerns will be addressed there.

In short, I highly recommend you read the *Now Purpose Manual* from cover to cover. This way *all* of the information is consumed. After finishing it, go back to the chapter, *How to Live Your Now Purpose*, and begin taking the steps.

All in all, the way you use this book is up to you. Please don't give it too much credit. *And,* don't blame any lack of purpose that you may experience on this book. The best way to get the most out of the *Manual* is to go into it with a sense of culpability. *You* are the main person responsible for your life. This book is merely a tool. It is my will that you use it to build a more satisfying and purposeful life.

But, first…

When is your purpose? NOW!

8 KEYS TO LIVING YOUR *NOW PURPOSE*

Welcome to your personal journey within! For this ride, you don't even have to strap on your seatbelt. Just open your mind to the possibility of discovering your truth and prepare to take the steps necessary to live an incredible life!

This chapter serves as the foundation for you to live your *Now Purpose*. Each of the keys discussed in this chapter will help you focus on the now like never before! It is through these keys that you will unlock the hidden treasure you've been seeking and you're likely to discover that it has been right in front of you all along. We all have something locked inside us ready to be born. For some, it may be a book or a YouTube channel. For others, it may be to develop a healthier lifestyle or become more emotionally secure. Ensuring that you're in alignment with the 8 keys outlined in this chapter will significantly increase your likelihood of discovering and beginning to *live* your *Now Purpose*.

Are you ready to UNLOCK your purpose?

yes!

Let's roll up our sleeves and get to work!

Key #1 - Awareness Leads to Purpose

It is challenging to figure out where you're going if you're unsure of where you are. Awareness is the ability to know things. The *thing* you must be aware of most is yourself. Self-awareness is the foundation to life. Your life is like a book and your book is the best story you can read because you are one-of-a-kind. Truth be told, you really aren't *finding* your purpose, you're just becoming more aware of it. To increase your self-awareness, it is helpful to ask yourself the following questions:

- What are my personality traits?
- What's the plot or theme in my story?
- Who are my adversaries?
- What challenges me?
- What motivates me?
- What are my strengths?
- What beliefs do I have?
- What fears do I have?
- What are my likes and dislikes?

Pay particular attention to the answers to these questions as they are critical for self-knowledge. This awareness will ultimately lead you to your purpose.

Think about anything you do with some level of confidence. You *know* you can do it. You *know* where your strengths lie. You're aware of the environment. You *know* you can complete the task. The key is to be aware of what brings you true fulfillment and purpose.

You are reading this book because you are aware that some aspect of your life is not quite where you'd like for it to be. You may or may not be sure of what it is, but you know that something is "off" with you right now. This sense of "off-ness" is the result of not feeling purposeful in one or more areas in your life. This awareness of lack is replaced with hope when you shift your consciousness to move in the direction of your purpose. In other words, you must accept that which has already been given before you are able to receive your desires.

I can assure you that your purpose is right in front of you. Increasing your awareness reveals this truth to you. *Now Purpose Manual* will only confirm what you already know. Allow yourself to unlock the magic that is inside you. Become aware of who you are. Know thyself.

Key #2 - Purpose = Do's and Don'ts

In life, there are two choices --- *do* and *don't*. Either we do things or we don't. We either have or have not. We either say, "Yes," or we say, "No." It's really that simple. This polarity of action and inaction is what I call Lights of Awareness™. Whenever you say, "Yes," or decide to do something, you simultaneously decide *not* to do something else. For example, if you have a job, you are not unemployed. If you are away in college, then you are not at home or wherever else you would be. If you are married, you are not single. You see? What you opt to do in any given moment, automatically eliminates the polar opposite.

As you discover your *Now Purpose* and begin to live it, you will inevitably encounter the various Lights of

Awareness. At varying points, the Lights will shine for you by triggering an emotional response that indicates how you should proceed in action. The Lights appear to bring your attention to your choices. It is your responsibility to heed their signal when they appear and respond in the manner that is most productive.

To get a better understanding of your Lights of Awareness™, ask yourself:

• What is it that I am currently DOING that is purposeful that I want to do more? (Green Lights)
• What do I need to SLOW down and not do as much? (Yellow Lights)
• What do I want to STOP doing for a reason? (Red Lights) *meaningless sex*
• What should I START doing that I'm currently not doing? (Black Lights) *Focus on school, I guess?*

Purposeful living is simply doing something on purpose or deciding not to do something for a reason. What you're doing or not doing may not seem that significant, but it's where you are. The present moment is what you should always be focused on.

Key #3 - Focus on *NOW*

In my work as a Spiritual Teacher, I've found that the reason people don't live their purpose in the now is because they see it as something that will be fulfilled in the future. This is why I don't use the words "life purpose" too often. For some reason, the *life* part makes it seem like something in the future or simply overwhelming or too big to be achieved or pursued right now.

Rest assured that you have everything you need to live your purpose today. Your purpose will change as you evolve, but that doesn't negate the fact that you are built to live in the moment. Do you think a professional weightlifter is lifting the same amount of weights as their first day? Absolutely not! They started where they were to get to where they are. You have everything you need to get the job done *right now*. Don't allow excuses to cloud your current situation making up reasons you need to wait until you get x, y or z before you can actively pursue your goals. This sort of behavior keeps your dreams on the back burner. Do you really want to keep waiting for things to fall perfectly into place before you go after your dreams? I didn't think so.

I know it can be difficult to stay in the current moment when it seems as if you're so far away from your ultimate vision of yourself. I get it. As a highly intuitive person, I've been given future visions of myself several times. In 2016, Sanserae and I hosted the first annual Soul Glow Spiritual Retreat. What's so special about that? I had a vision of it more than 5 years before it happened. I even shared the vision with my cousins, Orlando and Juice, along with other spiritual family. When I receive visions of things to come, I instantly place them on the back burner. If what I'm doing today is in alignment, then I know I'm heading in the right direction.

These are the questions you want to ask yoursel. _ day, especially when you feel like it's hard to remain focused in the current moment:

- What am I doing right now?
- Is it in alignment with my end result or goal?
- Am I doing something for it every day?

Your purpose is *now*. Period. Train yourself to see it this way. It will make your life a lot easier. Stress comes when we project into the future. The future has endless possibilities. Many of these possibilities are seemingly beyond your physical control. The now is way more manageable. You're already living in this moment, so you may as well start here.

Key #4 – Focus on What You Can Control

Let's face it. Some things are out of our control. This is where acceptance comes in. You must accept that which you cannot change. Fortunately, most things in our lives are fixable or we have a good amount of influence over them.

There are many situations in your life you have full domain over. One of the problems I often see people struggle with is worrying about things they have no control over. It's hard to live a more purpose-filled life when you're focused on things you can't do anything about. Worrying is wasting energy and engaging in it often is a recipe for mental distress and dis-ease.

Some desires we have control over are career changes, health choices, the quality of our relationships, spiritual orientation or practices, leisure activities, etc. Notice how you can do something about them? You have a major part to play in the outcome.

Then, there are personal things we have to accept that, for the most part, there is NOTHING we can do about. Some things we must accept and be at peace with are height, skin color, parents, birth place, facial appearance, disabilities, inabilities, etc. You pretty much have no control over these things.

Likewise, there are world situations that you can rally and protest against, but you have no direct control over them. Some worldwide conditions like racism, poverty, politics, religion, sexism, rape, murder and such are out of your hands to influence or reform on a global scale.

This key is not meant to stop you from doing what is in your heart. The aforementioned worldwide conditions are being fought by organizations every day. However, I caution anyone spending a great deal of energy in places wherein they can't make a significant difference. It's more impactful to join or start an organization that is actively working to reform things rather than to rant and complain on social media about how messed up things are. Don't get me wrong. I'm not suggesting that larger scale issues aren't important. Nor am I saying that such work can't be purposeful. I'm simply suggesting that there may be other ways that your energy can make a greater impact. Think about where and how your energy can be best spent and focus it there. Take it for what it's worth and let your heart decide.

As you uncover your Lights of Awareness, make sure to include things you can physically do. These Lights are action steps. The purpose of the Lights is to bring awareness to things you can do or should not be doing. *You* must be the one in control.

Ask yourself the following questions to help you determine whether the issue you are facing allows you to have control and influence for your purpose, filling in the blank with the issue you are facing:

- Is there something I can physically do about ____?
- Is my purpose of ____ within my control for the most part?
- Am I really able to ____?

If your answer was no to any of the questions, I would advise avoiding that direction, but, if you're feeling daring, you may travel that path at your own risk. The takeaway from this key is to put more energy toward things you are confident that you can do something about. This approach will increase your overall quality of life and help you be and feel more purposeful and productive.

Key #5 - It's All About YOU

Knowing that you have everything you need to live your *Now Purpose* extends to those around you, as well. Too many people think they need someone else's validation or assistance to fulfill their mission or purpose. Yes, it may prove to be helpful to have someone's assistance, but a lack of help is not the reason you're feeling empty or as if you're not living your purpose. It's imperative that you know that you are good enough to do what you need to do. It's all about you! If you do not have the help you think you need, then you must not need it today. Situations will change as you progress on your path. The current situation is the most important one.

Do your best to avoid allowing your mind to create barriers that aren't there. Your ego will tell you that you cannot do it. The way to combat this overactive voice is to simply *do you*. Do what you are capable of. You have the power because you *are* the power.
Trust and faith in yourself is all you need to get started. If another person or resource is required for your purpose, you would already have it or they will show up shortly. You must act to attract!

To determine if you're focusing on what you're capable of doing independently, ask yourself:

- What people do I have around me right now?
- What resources do I have?
- What natural talents do I have?
- What skills have I acquired?

16

You learned in Key #4 to focus on what *you* can control and to avoid wasting your energy. This concept also applies to WAITING for someone to show up in your life. Why wait? What can YOU do NOW? Train yourself to become more self-sustained. Not only will this effort help you to reach your goals, but it will also inspire and empower others to begin to show up to help you on *your* mission.

Key #6 – Know Your *Now Purpose* Area of Development

Life can be divided into several major areas --- finances, relationships, family, business, personal development, health, spirituality and fun. Each area of life is important, but determining which to prioritize development in at a given time is equally important. When should you be more focused on health over relationships? When is spirituality a priority over fun and entertainment? This differs for each person. We all have life cycles. Knowing your life cycle will help you determine when a specific area of life should be a focal point. The best way to determine your life cycle is to feel where your heart is pulling you. This pull will lead you to the appropriate development area for your *Now Purpose*.

The area of life you feel most drawn to develop will reflect where you are on your path. For instance, an extremely healthy and wealthy person may not be called to make their finances and physical fitness more purposeful. Rather, they may not feel a strong spiritual connection which will direct their focus to grow spiritually. Conversely, a spiritually-evolved soul may be drawn to get their finances in order or build stronger relationships. Your *Now Purpose* development area is all about what you should be doing now for that particular aspect of your life. The key is to avoid allowing others to dictate YOUR motives and actions. Your purpose is to live YOUR life. Not someone else's perception of reality. Trust yourself to know which area is best for you to focus on.

Key #7 – Know How to Take Action

It's one thing to know your purpose. It's another thing to know how you're going to achieve it. Many get stuck in analysis paralysis because they lack an action plan. Without a map, it's difficult to travel. The reason most people never achieve what they want is because they don't know how they're going to get there. How can you get to step 10 without knowing steps 1-9? How can you live your purpose without having things to do? You must know *HOW* you are going to achieve your goals. To find out your action steps, ask the question, *"How?"*

Ask yourself:

- How am I going to get ___?
- How am I going to get more ___?
- How am I going to have less ___?
- How am I going to stop ___?
- How am I going to start ___?

- How am I going to do ____ more?
- How am I going to do ____ less?

Once you have an idea or direction for your purpose, you'll want to know how to achieve it. What are the specific steps you must take to get to your destination? What actions or inaction will lead you to your desired outcome? As you uncover your Lights of Awareness and answer your, *"How?"* questions, you will see actionable steps fall into place right in front of you.

The main reason most don't seek the action steps to live out their purpose is because it's easier to say you want to do something than to actually *do* it. Whenever something lives in your head or mind only, it stays a fantasy or dream. Dreams only come to life with action. These actions are the answers to your, *"How?"* questions. If you ask yourself "How?" enough, the action steps will reveal themselves.

Key #8 – Strengthen Your Motivating Desire by Asking, "Why?"

The absolute most important question to ask yourself is, *"Why?"* The word, *why,* is a trigger that enflames desire and motivation. When your desires are strong enough, you will change or do *anything.* Your *why* is the fuel to drive your *Now Purpose.* Without a strong enough *why,* it's almost impossible to accomplish anything, especially when change is required.

Take a moment to think about the things that you really *don't* want to do. You tend to do these things because your *why* or desire for the payoff is stronger than your disdain for the act itself. You may hate your job but you strongly want to pay your bills and keep the lights on. The desire to live with electricity and maintain your lifestyle is stronger than the mundane grind of a 9 to 5. Another example of having a strong *why* is with health. Every day, people do something they may not enjoy like jogging, eating healthy, working out, etc. The act of being healthy may not be fun or exciting but the end-result is highly desirable. The desire, or *why*, outweighs the "work." When your *why* is stronger than the work, you will be motivated to do anything.

I'm convinced that you know your purpose or calling and just refuse to commit. If it was easy, you'd probably be doing it. You avoid starting or continuing because it's hard. You haven't created a strong enough desire to push you past your will of complacency. Will is temporary. A strong reason for your desire is long-term.

To strengthen your desire, ask yourself:

- Why do I want to get ___?
- Why do I want to have more ___?
- Why do I want to have less ___?
- Why do I want to stop ___?
- Why do I want to start ___?
- Why do I want to do ___ more?
- Why do I want to do ___ less?

Just as you asked yourself, "How," you want to ask yourself "Why," multiple times to get to your real desire. We all have hidden desires and *whys* for everything in our lives. When you probe yourself by repeatedly asking, "Why," you will get to the root of your desires. This root desire will ultimately be a major catalyst for change in your life.

LIGHTS OF AWARENESS™

The Lights of Awareness™ is a tool that will help you get a clearer understanding of your *Now Purpose*. It's the ultimate method for conducting a self-inventory that is beneficial for your soul. It provides clarity and reduces the tendency to make excuses. As a Spiritual Teacher, I've found that the main excuse people make pertaining to pursuing their purpose is being uncertain of what to do or where to start. The *Lights of Awareness* model will help you become clear on the things to do and how to begin. It is a model that encourages you to be honest with yourself and become more aware of how you feel. If this model is followed explicitly and, you are open and honest throughout the process, you will benefit greatly and receive more light and insight into your *Now Purpose*.

A Light is an action or inaction that is purposeful. Lights of Awareness is about becoming conscious of our unspoken motives and the decisions we make as a result. What you believe to be your purpose will be revealed by the Lights. As indicated in the chapter, *8 Keys to Living Your Now Purpose*, the most important aspect to keep in mind when shedding light on your awareness is to stay focused on the present moment. Do your best not to allow your thoughts to drift and/or project into the future. Remember, your purpose is *NOW*. In order to find purpose in the now, you must be consciously aware of the present moment.

Let's apply this to a real-life scenario. When you are driving and approach an intersection with traffic lights, you know to stop at a red light, slow down at a yellow one, and go when the signal is green. At the moment you arrive in the intersection, these lights become important. As a human being, we approach intersections in life every day. Only, instead of calling those cross-points intersections, we call them decisions. There are things we know that we should be doing. When we have this degree of clarity, that we should be engaged in a particular behavior or activity, it is similar to being in that intersection again and the traffic signal gives us a green light telling us to go. There are also times when we are doing things that we know we need to slow down on just like when we approach a yellow light in an intersection. When there are things we are doing that we feel like we should stop doing, that's just like life giving us a big, bright red light. Finally, there are black lights. These lights show up for us when we realize that there are things we know that we should start doing, but we are not currently doing them.

Every day, you think about the things you want to do more of (Green Lights) or things you want to start (Black Lights). Then, there are the things you no longer want to do (Red Lights) or not do as much (Yellow Lights). This process is subconsciously created and looped through our daily action or inaction until the cycle of behavior is broken. As you focus on your Lights, you will tap into your awareness and begin to shine light on these things. Whenever you shine light on something, it will create darkness in other areas. This analogy is akin to focusing on what you know you should be doing and letting the rest be in the background. There will be times when you want to shine light on your relationships and family. Other times, you may be focused on your career and finances. All aspects of your life are important and you will always have responsibilities to maintain balance in those areas but, if you are honest you know that every aspect of your life cannot be prioritized at the same time.

In order to effectively use the *Lights of Awareness*, you must focus on what *you* see to be right for you today rather than what society, family, and others may tell you is right for you. Only *you* can live your life, so only *you* should decide what is right for you at any given time. Make sure to be and remain in the driver's seat. Depending on age or the current life cycle you are experiencing, some pressures may come into play regarding things that could or should have already been accomplished. Accept that we may make mistakes but, these do not have to prevent us from moving forward. Life is ever-evolving and most setbacks, if chosen to view them as such, are small when viewed through the scope of your overall lifetime. Sometimes, a step or two backwards is necessary in order to progress two or more steps in the right direction.

The fact that there are specific things you need to shine light on is the basis of the *Lights of Awareness*. Everything in your life is not equal. Regardless of whether your family, relationships, or even career seem that they should be more important, you may be drawn to focus on another area of your life more intently like finances or leisure. If you continue to deny the *Lights* you should be focused on, other areas of life can be adversely impacted. Have you ever known someone who works many hours because it's the only way they see to provide for their family despite their burning desire to start a business and travel the world with their family? Even though they continue to do something they see as right, it will likely have a detrimental effect on the quality of their relationships. We all know people who get off work grouchy and sometimes, take it out on others.

The power to know which *Lights* to focus on and when to focus on them is a skill within itself. For some, it may come easily, but others may have to work to develop the skill. Whether it comes easily to you or you have to put forth a bit more effort, you will dramatically increase the odds of feeling more purposeful by becoming more aware of your *Lights* and the messages they bring.

Let's take a closer look at the *Lights of Awareness* and their messages.

GREEN LIGHTS

Message: *"More, please!"*

Green Lights are the things we can't get enough of because we see them as something that benefits us. We want to do more of these things because, for the most part, it's enjoyable and adds to the quality of our lives.

Ever since I was a child, I always wanted to own my own business. The concept of working for someone else for the rest of my life depressed me. When I got my first taste of entrepreneurship as a seller on eBay, it immediately had me craving more. Starting businesses became one of my Green Lights. I started my eBay career with three movies. The movies were *The Blob*, *Godzilla vs. Smog Monster* and *Five Deadly Venoms*. After steady sales, I wanted to add more titles. So, adding more movie titles became a Green Light. As things progressed with my business, more Green Lights, or things I wanted more of, began to show up for me. I found that I wanted more help with receiving and shipping inventory, so I got a business partner. I wanted more freedom from my regular job at the time and I ended up having to work only 4 days per week, then that reduced to 2. I wanted to increase my profit margin, so I found a new supplier with lower wholesale prices, and when I wanted more exposure to my listings, I created an eBay store and refined my targeted keywords so that my products were easier for consumers to find.

Green Lights will differ for each person. They will also pertain to the most focused on area of life. The key is to be honest with yourself about what you want more of and the things you want to do more often. Most times, these things will have a positive impact on your life. Other times, it's just something you enjoy or like having. Regardless, it's about fulfilling your *Now Purpose,* so your heart is the best judge.

YELLOW LIGHTS

Message: *"Caution ahead!"*

Have something but want less of it? Doing something but want to slow down or not do it as often? Yellow Lights are the things we don't want to stop doing altogether, but definitely want to slow down how much or how often we do them. Yellow Lights may be the trickiest to determine. As humans, we usually think in polarizing ways. We either think we should do something or not do something. We rarely consider frequency and intensity, but the middle ground of not doing as much or having less of something may be a sweet spot to explore.

Normally, you want less of something you may not need. Sometimes, it may appear you need these things on the surface level. Take a job or, the way you make your money for instance. You may *feel* like you need it but don't want to do as much. Working less hours becomes a Yellow Light. Some Yellow Lights are not what most people consider beneficial but, for whatever reason, letting it go is difficult. A few examples of things you may want to do less of are drinking coffee, smoking cigarettes, gambling or drinking alcohol. This is not to say you want to indulge in said vice for the rest of your life but, you are not yet interested in stopping the behavior at this point.

Yellow Lights have the tendency to manipulate our better judgment when they appear as vices and addictions. The ability to consistently distinguish the Yellow Lights from the Red Lights is a sign of emerging self-awareness.

Yellow Lights can also be things we want to do less often because we want more of something else. For example, if you want to spend more time with your partner on Friday, then you will have to spend less time with your friends on the weekend or less time working on Friday to clear your schedule for your loved one. In this example, Yellow Lights help to free up other parts of your life so that you can spend more time doing things that are more desirable.

RED LIGHTS

Message: *"Danger lurks!"*

Do you need to stop doing something? Need to get rid of something in your life completely? Red Lights are the things that we know no longer serve us. These are the things you want or need to stop doing. Every time you approach a Red Light, you have an ill feeling of emptiness in the pit of your stomach. You know you no longer want to do these things. You're over it already! Your Red Lights are likely the ones you think about most often. Red Lights are easy to detect because we know they are hindering us from our highest good.

Unlike the vices mentioned in Yellow Lights, Red Lights are the ones you don't want to partake in anymore at all.

Instead of slowing down on said vice, you are *ready to quit!*

Anything you want to quit, stop, or no longer have/need are Red Lights. Some examples of Red Lights or, things you may want to give up completely, are credit card debt, a job so you can start a business, procrastinating, unhealthy food choices, cheating, lying, stealing, etc. Pay attention to the actions and things that prevent you from going to the next level. These obstacles are usually cloaked Red Lights.

BLACK LIGHTS

Message: *"Let's get it cracking!"*

Black Lights are the most foreign to us because we have no personal experience with them. These are the things we want to start doing or are the things we want to have but currently do not.

The Black Lights are only things with which you have no personal reference. Because you have never had them, you can't possibly know what they entail. Because you've never done it, you don't know what it's like. Black Lights usually will come as that voice in the back of your head that tells you what you should start doing. This direction usually gets denied because it's telling you to do something unknown. If the suggestions are not put into action, this nudging voice causes anxiety and frustration. Left to linger too long, we eventually experience regret and dissatisfaction with life.

Black Lights often feel like a gamble because you have no past experience with them. This may cause you to be cautious and hold off on starting something new. It's easier to continue doing something we're used to doing than to try something new. This is definitely the case with very conservative people.

Giving more attention to what's been nagging at you is a good way to discover your Black Lights. Some common Black Lights are writing a book, public speaking, traveling to a foreign land, meditating, exercising, or starting a new business. These things may seem big and intimidating which is why most don't accomplish them.

Just like the others, your Black Lights will be unique to you. There is no right or wrong. Be obedient and listen to your Spirit.

Lights of Awareness™ Examples

The chart below provides an operational view of how the *Lights of Awareness* can show up in daily living. In our example, this individual desires to increase their productivity, adopt a healthier and more active lifestyle, and improve their financial standing. The chart displays how the *Lights* would appear and what actions should take place in order for this person to feel more fulfilled.

GREEN (more)	YELLOW (less)	RED (stop)	BLACK (start)
Exercising more	Only working out legs	Stop missing scheduled workout days	Start jogging and running and working other muscle groups
Being more productive	Less time surfing the internet and social media	Stop replying to emails first thing in the morning	Start writing a book
Adopting a healthier lifestyle	Drinking less alcohol	Stop eating pork and sugary foods	Begin taking supplements and eating more veggies
Having more money accessible	Spending less money on clothes and entertainment	Stop going to the movie theatre and renting movies	Start watching movies on Netflix, saving a specified amount each pay period and looking into making sound financial investments

HOW TO LIVE YOUR *NOW PURPOSE*

In this chapter, you will learn the step-by-step process to discover your *Now Purpose* and begin living it! Each step provides detailed actions and when executed as indicated, will be useful in the process of finding deeper meaning in any area of life.

Step #1: Choose an area of life you feel drawn to make more purposeful.

The first step to finding your *Now Purpose* is to identify the area of life you wish to make more meaningful. Because purpose is unique to each individual, the area of life selected will be different for everyone. The area of life you choose to focus upon may also change depending on what life cycle you're in. For instance, when you are 20 years old, your prioritized area of life is likely to be different than when you are 80 years old. At 20, you may be more focused on relationships and career, while, at 80, you would likely be seeking more leisure and fun in your life. The areas of life differ because our needs and desires change significantly throughout our various life cycles.

The first key to finding your *Now Purpose*, taught you that awareness leads to purpose. The more aware you are, the more purposeful you will be. With this, discovering the area of life your soul is leading you to place your focus upon is essential to finding your *Now Purpose*.

The primary areas of life are as follows:

- Spirituality
- Business/Career
- Finances
- Physical Health
- Mental & Emotional Health
- Family
- Relationships
- Personal Development
- Leisure & Fun

One or more of the areas of life may tug at your heart. You may have activities or major roles in each area of life, but there is likely to be one or two that *REALLY* call you. Remember, our purpose is *now*, so you will be drawn to one of the areas of life more for fulfillment *today*. This awareness will also reduce the stress of finding your purpose through the process of elimination. You can also see how different areas were focal points at different times of your life. Right now, you may be focused on your business or career whereas five years ago, it may have been relationships and family. Ten years ago, you may have been more focused on leisure and fun. This will likely change in the future as well. Five years from now, you may be totally focused on your money to secure investments in preparation for retirement. In another 15 years, family and friends may become the priority as you may have more free time on your hands. In a nutshell, time works like this: The past is meant for reflection and learning, and while the future is not guaranteed, we still spend time planning for it. The present moment is all we ever really have. Since we're living in it, the only time we should be focused on is now.

Step #2: Gain greater awareness in your chosen area of life.

After you've chosen the area of life you wish to make more purposeful, you then want to become more aware, in general. Much is revealed when you take a conscious inventory of your life. This evolving self-inventory denotes true self-awareness.

Asking yourself the right questions is essential to getting the answers that will lead you to learning more about your chosen area of life. I refer to these inquiries as *awareness questions*. These questions are meant to make you more conscious of yourself, your thoughts, ideas and choices, ultimately leading to self-awareness.

Asking yourself the questions listed below will aid in discovering which area of life you should prioritize.

General Awareness Questions:

- What are my likes?
- What are my dislikes?
- Where do my interests lie?
- What triggers my emotions (desire, fear, anger, joy, sadness, frustration, etc.)?

34

- What are my personal strengths (talents, skills, abilities)?
- What aspects of myself would I like to develop more (challenges, obstacles, blocks, limitations, etc.)?
- What are my personal beliefs (opinions, morals, assumptions)?
- What motivates me?
- What inspires me?
- What are my most common thoughts?
- Am I more employee-minded or entrepreneur-minded?
- Do I learn best by reading, listening, watching or through practical, hands-on experience?
- Do I communicate best by writing, speaking or via physical demonstration?
- Am I more extroverted or introverted? Does this change in various settings? If so, when/where?
- What time(s) of day am I most productive --- morning, afternoon, evening and/or late night?
- In which season(s) of the year am I most productive --- spring, summer, fall and/or winter?

Depending on which area of life you seek to make more purposeful, the awareness will change. For instance, there are different sets of awareness needed for family than leisure and fun. The same can be said for all areas of life. You will notice in the subsequent chapters that there are varying questions specific to each of the identified areas of life.

Step #3: Know your Lights of Awareness™.

After you gain a greater understanding of your focused area of life, it's time to identify your Lights of Awareness. As discussed earlier, your Lights of Awareness will lead you straight to your *Now Purpose*. Be sure you provide as many answers as possible. The more Lights you have brightening your path, the more identifiable action steps you will have for each selected area of life.

Ask yourself the questions listed below pertaining to your chosen area of life.

Lights of Awareness Questions:

Green Lights
• What are you *currently* doing that you want to do more?

Yellow Lights
• What are you *currently* doing that you want to do less?

Red Lights
• What do you want to completely *stop* doing?

Black Lights
• What do you want to *start* doing?

Step #4: Select the Light that feels heaviest on your heart and mind.

Your *Now Purpose* will be something you either wish to do or have more or less of *or* something that you wish to stop altogether. The Lights of Awareness helps to expose these desires. Now, it's time to select one of the Lights to examine. It doesn't matter which color you choose first, but it is advisable that you select the one that's heaviest on your heart. This is the one that is going to help you feel most purposeful.

After you've answered the applicable questions and your Lights of Awareness are shining, you may notice that there are some things you mentioned more than once. There's a great chance that this will lead you to one Light in particular. It's usually the thing that keeps repeating itself that points directly to what we should be doing.

It is most beneficial to select one Light to begin with so that you are able to hone your focus on one targeted area. Most people become overwhelmed when they are faced with too much responsibility. The less you have diverting your attention, the more likely you will be to feel the task is feasible and actually *do* what you can to work toward its fulfillment. Always remember that one comes before two. Starting with just one Light is not only more logical, it makes the process less daunting and quite a bit simpler.

Step #5: Identify your action steps.

If you answer the questions pertaining to your Lights of Awareness specifically enough, you should get clarity on the actionable steps you can take to begin living your *Now Purpose*. The more you ask yourself, *"How?"* the more action steps you will get.

Without action steps, it's difficult to achieve *anything*. Do yourself a favor and make sure you know how you're going to accomplish your *Now Purpose*.

Here are some *"How?"* questions you can ask yourself to produce actionable steps toward your *Now Purpose*:

- How am I going to get ___?
- How am I going to get rid of ___?
- How am I going to start doing ___?
- How am I going to stop doing ___?
- How am I going to do less ___?
- How am I going to have more ___?
- How am I going to have less ___?

Step #6: Find your motivating desire.

This very well could be the most important step even if it doesn't appear to be on the surface. The problem is we tend to pay too much attention to the surface or cover instead of the content within. You can know what you want to do and how you're going to do it, but without a strong desire, or a reason *why*, you may not do anything to reach your goal.

This was illustrated very clearly for me when my first book, *Deity Linkage Manual: How to Find Your Gods & Goddesses Using Numerology*, was released in 2015. Prior to then, I had wanted to write a book for years. I had even started writing a few. It wasn't until I divinely *"received"* the formula for linking deities to Numerology that I felt genuinely compelled to share the information in the form of a book. I had a burning desire to have this powerful intellectual property protected and I wanted the world to be able to benefit from the information. As a result, the system has helped *thousands*! This desire to share became a motivating factor for me to write what ultimately became an Amazon #1 Bestseller in *multiple categories*! Oh yeah, and did I mention that I wrote *Deity Linkage Manual* in one week? Yes, an entire book that has changed thousands of lives in *one week*! This proves that possibilities are endless when one's motivation is strong enough.

To find *your* motivating desire, simply ask yourself, *"Why?"* Keep asking yourself, *"Why?"* until you get an answer that propels you into action.

Here are some *"Why?"* questions to help you find your motivation:

- Why do I want to get ___?
- Why do I want to get rid of ___?
- Why do I want to start doing ___?
- Why do I want to stop doing ___?
- Why do I want to do less ___?

- Why do I want to have more ___?
- Why do I want to have less ___?

Step #7: Act *NOW!*

What's the use in knowing what you want to do and how you're going to do it if you don't actually *DO IT*? You must *act* to really shine your Light. Whatever actions you develop in step #5, are your starting points to moving into your *Now Purpose*. Those are the things you want to begin doing right away.

Some Lights may require you to act more than once. Don't become discouraged by the repetition. Very few goals are accomplished with just one attempt. The more you do, the less you'll overthink and discourage yourself from pursuing your goal. Moreover, if one of your Lights is something you've been neglecting or avoiding for some time, I strongly suggest that you act even faster! The longer you procrastinate on something you really want to do, the less likely you are to do it. Remember, these efforts are for your benefit. The sooner you put these steps into action, the faster you'll experience the fruits of your labor. The best time to act is today! Don't hesitate. Act *now*!

Step #8: Keep a journal.

To ensure you are on track and to add some accountability, keep a running log of your progress in a journal. You can maintain a journal on your electronic device or use a regular notebook. The point is to record all of your activities and keep notes of anything that occurs in the process of pursuing your *Now Purpose*. Some things you may want to include in your journal are:

- A scheduled time for working with your Light(s)
- A summary of actions you've performed
- Helpful tips, research or inspirations you've discovered pertaining to your goal
- Notes or thoughts based on the actions you've performed
- Future ideas and plans
- To-do lists
- Photos or visual aids that motivate you
- An outline of your larger vision or a description of what you're currently doing that will help you to reach future goals

Maintaining this information in a journal or running log will be a helpful way to monitor your progress toward your *Now Purpose* as well as recording your thoughts, ideas and plans. Keep the journal with you so that you can easily record your inspirations as they occur. Doing this frequently will reinforce your positive behavior by providing a written track record of your successes while simultaneously allowing you to closely examine areas in which you wish to make improvements.

Step #9: Review and repeat.

The final step in the process is to review your journal on a regular basis. I recommend that you set aside a time every day for this review. This will keep you focused and ensure that your Lights and all of your action steps remain in the forefront of your mind.

You also want to repeat the actions that need to be done more than once on a routine basis. As discussed earlier, many Lights will require you to do something more than once like meditating, exercising, eating healthy, focusing on positive thoughts, etc. Make sure you establish a solid practice involving such activities. This sort of repetition will lead to your desired achievement.

Once you have completed all action steps for your Light, revisit step #1 and start again. Choose something new to focus on and to make your life even more purposeful.

The next 9 chapters define each area of life and discuss why it is important to find more meaning in each. Each chapter is designed to walk you through the first 6 steps to help you find your *Now Purpose*. You will answer awareness questions and determine your Lights in that specific area of life. There are examples along the way for each question and Light and you will also be prompted to develop your action steps and motivating desire. And for an *additional* push toward your *Now Purpose*, there's an activity you can complete for each respected area of life. Finish the exercise to gain even greater awareness!

You may choose to jump to the section that correlates with your focused area of life *or* you can read each chapter to determine which one of them resonates with you the most. As discussed previously, whichever area you feel a strong connection with will be the one you should focus on first.

NOW PURPOSE IN
SPIRITUALITY

Spirituality is our connection and interaction with the Source and the unseen world. To be spiritual means you are aware of or believe in something beyond the physical. It is the opposite of the mundane and secular. Spirituality is the process by which you choose to develop your soul.

Spirituality also relates to one's expression of their innate spiritual gifts and abilities. Ask any psychic, medium, healer or diviner whether they are "spiritual," and I bet you'll get a confirming answer. It's a widely accepted fact that humans have intuition and subtle energy. All that is unseen and inexplicable can be viewed as spiritual. This includes our intuitive thoughts and subtle energy that influence our feelings or vibrations.

As you grow spiritually, you may be drawn to specific practices like meditation, yoga, charity work, philanthropy, etc. You may seek opportunities to expand your spiritual practice with like-minded people by joining a church, a mosque or a metaphysical group or program. You may also find yourself intrigued by metaphysical and esoteric subjects such as crystals, Numerology, Tarot, chakras, etc. and begin studying them intently.

Finding your purpose in Spirituality can lead you to new people, places, practices and tools. This is a very vast and encompassing area of life, so do not get frustrated if your Lights don't seem too "spiritual."

As you answer the questions, take notice of anything you may have mentioned more than once. More than likely, those responses will help you work more productively with your Lights of Awareness.

Awareness Questions for Spirituality

What do you like about your current spiritual path?
(Examples: Reading spiritual books, going to church, fellowship with like-minded souls, loving the Creator, etc.)

_____

_____

_____

_____

What do you dislike?
(Examples: Not meditating enough, never having seen angels, dislike for my church, my altar setup and location, etc.)

_____

_____

_____

Do you have any fears about spirituality?
(Examples: That there is no God, fear of going to hell, falling off my path, never finding a true teacher, etc.)

_____

_____

_____

_____

_____

Do you have any frustrations with spirituality?
(*Examples: That people charge for spiritual services, sexism, people preaching at my front door, when my child interrupts my meditation, etc.*)

_____

_____

_____

What aspect of your spiritual practice brings you the most joy?
(*Examples: Giving my ancestors offerings, a feeling of oneness, knowing I have a Creator, playing with my tarot cards, etc.*)

_____

_____

_____

What do you want most from your spiritual path?
(*Examples: To be able to levitate, increased intuition, to astral project, find a spiritual community, etc.*)

_____

_____

_____

What are your strongest spiritual gifts, talents and/or abilities?

(Examples: Intuition, daily commitment, being able to share with others, dream recall, etc.)

_____
_____
_____
_____

What are your biggest challenges on your spiritual path?
(Examples: Meditating consistently, faith, trusting teachers, knowing where to start, etc.)

_____
_____
_____
_____

What are your current spiritual practices?
(Examples: Giving gratitude, keeping a dream journal, yoga, charitable contributions, etc.)

_____
_____
_____
_____

What are some beliefs or assumptions you have about spirituality that may be true or false?
(Examples: Angels are real, Oshun is my deity, my ancestors are not alive on the other side, there is no other side, etc.)

_____
_____
_____
_____

Take note of any items you may have mentioned more than once. It is likely, they will help with your Lights of Awareness.

Lights of Awareness in Spirituality

As you work to identify your Lights, be certain to respond to the questions with as much specificity as possible. The more detail you add to your responses, the more clarity you will gain in determining your *Now Purpose*. The key is to focus on identifying *actionable items* or things that you can physically *DO*.

Green Lights

What are you currently doing on your spiritual path but know you should do MORE of?
(Examples: Meditating, trusting my teacher, giving ancestral offerings, studying and practicing Numerology, etc.)

_____
_____
_____
_____

Yellow Lights

What are you currently doing that YOU feel like you should SLOW DOWN or not do as much?
(Examples: Spending time with people who are not like-minded or not on a spiritual journey of any kind, watching TV programs that may not be appropriate or have too much violence, sharing my opinion with others even if they didn't ask, etc.)

48

_____

_____

_____

_____

Red Lights

What are you currently doing that YOU know you should STOP doing on your spiritual path?
(Examples: Eating pork, cursing, being dishonest, stealing, etc.)

_____

_____

_____

_____

Black Lights

What do you feel like you SHOULD BE doing that you're currently not doing on your spiritual path?
(Examples: Studying Astrology, donating or tithing, practicing magick, keeping a dream journal, etc.)

_____

_____

_____

_____

Identify Your Action Steps in Spirituality (How?)

Review what you have written above, then select one of your Lights. Which of your Lights feels heaviest on your heart?
(Example: Practicing magick)

_____
_____
_____
_____

Ask yourself, "*HOW* am I going to achieve ____?"
(Example: Question – How am I going to learn to practice magick? Answer – By studying a system of magick.)

_____
_____
_____
_____

Now, ask yourself "HOW?" again.
(Example: Question – How am I going to study a system of magick? Answer – By finding a system that resonates with me and buying a book on the subject.)

_____
_____
_____
_____

If still not clear on what to do based on your answer(s) or if you feel you need additional actionable steps, continue asking yourself, "*HOW?*"
(Example: Question - How am I going to find a system that resonates with me?
Answer - By searching Google for the most popular magical practices and getting a book on the one the feels best for me.)

_____

_____
_____
_____

Keep asking yourself, *"HOW?"* until you identify clearly defined ACTIONABLE answers.

Record the ACTION STEPS you identified on the lines below.

_____
_____
_____
_____
_____
_____
_____
_____

Find Your Motivating Desire in Spirituality (Why?)

When finding your motivating desire, be sure your justification is honest and authentic. With this, it's perfectly appropriate to give yourself permission to be extremely self-centered because your motivation is what will give you the fuel you need to change. The answers to your reasoning of, *"Why?"* are crucial to your transformation.

Ask yourself "WHY?" Why do I want to achieve ____? *(Example Question: Why do I want to practice magick? Answer: To have influence over my reality.)*

_____

_____

_____

_____

Now, ask yourself, *"WHY?"* again and record your response.
(Example Question: Why do I want to influence my reality? Answer: Because I do not like my current lifestyle.)

_____

_____

_____

_____

Ask yourself "WHY?" a third time and record your response.
(Example Question: Why do I dislike my lifestyle? Answer: Because I never seem to have money to do what I want.)

_____

_____

_____

_____

_____

Review the responses to your *"WHY?"* questions above and summarize them in a statement that makes sense to you. Record your statement on the lines below.
(Example: I want to effectively do magick to increase my abundance and prosperity.)

_____

_____

_____

_____

Mastering Masters Exercise

There are plenty of spiritual teachers and guides in the world. In the last century, the introduction of technological innovations such as television and the Internet have opened up a myriad of avenues for metaphysical and esoteric teachers to establish platforms and share their knowledge. There are also less mainstream spiritual teachers within our local communities that are equally as influential. Think about the spiritual teachers that have influenced you. Guided by the questions below, consider how these teachers have impacted your spiritual development. Completing this exercise will help you gain more clarity and find purpose on your spiritual path.

Record your responses to the items below on the lines provided.

Is there a teacher, living or transitioned, that had an impact on your life?

_____

_____

_____

_____

Who are your spiritual role models and why do you admire them?

_____
_____
_____
_____

Do you know of a person who demonstrates an ideal spiritual life?

_____
_____
_____
_____

What does this person do that benefits their spirituality?

_____
_____
_____
_____

Which of their spiritual practices would you be willing to adopt?

_____
_____
_____
_____

Choose one or more spiritual practices to add to your regimen and list them here. Feel free to make any adjustments to fit your unique personal needs and abilities.

_____

S. ALI MYERS

_____

_____

_____

NOW PURPOSE IN
BUSINESS/CAREER

Business is defined as a person's profession, occupation or trade. For many people, business or career is a major part of life. Most work for an average of 8 hours per day which is one-third of the 24-hour day. If you are investing *that* much time in this area of life, you probably want to make sure your job is aligned with your purpose.

Business can also be viewed as your calling, mission or purpose. Many of the clients I have worked with refer to their business or career when thinking about their purpose. What say you? Do *you* think about your livelihood or the way you make a living when thinking about your purpose or calling? More than likely you do.

Whether your career is your true calling or not, it's undeniable that it is a major aspect of your life. As mentioned in the first paragraph, you work for a large portion of your day. Anything that consumes *that* much of your time is a *big* piece of the puzzle of your life. Don't like the puzzle? Then make sure you're in alignment with your "puzzle pieces." Aligning with each "piece" guarantees your *peace* of mind.

In this chapter, the word business is used to describe your profession, job, career, mission, calling, etc. Feel free to replace the word business to best describe YOUR particular situation.

Awareness Questions for Business

What, if anything, do you like about your current business?
(Examples: The pay, freedom, hours, co-workers, etc.)

_____

_____

_____

_____

What do you dislike?
(Examples: Location, advancement opportunities, management, discrimination, etc.)

_____

_____

_____

_____

Do you have any fears associated with business?
(Examples: Not making enough money, not having enough for retirement, lack of quality time with loved ones, customers leaving me, etc.)

_____

_____

_____

_____

What frustrates you about business?
(Examples: unpredictable revenue, feeling like I'm competing with similar businesses, having to charge for my services, not knowing what to charge, etc.)

_____

_____
_____
_____

What do you want most from your business?
(Examples: To make an impact, to have a legacy, to make and/or receive steady charitable donations, stability, etc.)

_____
_____
_____
_____

What are your best business talents, skills and/or abilities?
(Examples: Intuition, web design, management, payroll, etc.)

_____
_____
_____
_____

What is most challenging for you?
(Examples: Communication skills, networking, technical abilities, fear of public speaking, etc.)

_____
_____
_____
_____

What are some beliefs or assumptions you have about business that may be true or false?

(Examples: It won't take long to be profitable, I'm getting laid off next year, my boss doesn't like me, I won't be able to find good employees, etc.)

_____

_____

_____

_____

Take note of any items you may have mentioned more than once. It is likely, they will help with your Lights of Awareness.

Lights of Awareness in Business

As you work to identify your Lights, be certain to respond to the questions with as much specificity as possible. The more detail you add to your responses, the more clarity you will gain in determining your *Now Purpose*. The key is to focus on identifying *actionable items* or things that you can physically *DO*.

Green Lights

What are you currently doing for business that you know you should do MORE of?
(Examples: Delegating, cold calling, planning, making YouTube videos, etc.)

_____

_____

_____

_____

Yellow Lights

What are you currently doing that YOU feel like you should SLOW DOWN or not do as much?
(Examples: Working long hours, bargain shopping for supplies, taking time off, refusing clients or assignments, etc.)

_____

_____

_____

_____

Red Lights

What are you currently doing that YOU know you should STOP doing as it relates to business?
(Examples: Stealing customers from friends, underpaying employees, playing small, procrastinating, etc.)

_____

_____

_____

_____

Black Lights

What do you feel like you SHOULD BE doing that you're currently NOT doing as it pertains to business?
(Examples: Adding inventory, marketing to a specific demographic, customer appreciation days, creating a website, etc.)

_____

_____

_____

_____

Identify Your Action Steps in Business (How?)

Review what you have written above, then select one of your Lights. Which of your Lights feels heaviest on your heart?
(Example: Creating a website)

_____

_____

_____

_____

Ask yourself, "HOW am I going to achieve _____?"
(Example: Question – How am I going to create a website? Answer – By hiring someone to design it.)

_____

_____

_____

_____

Now, ask yourself, "HOW?" again.
(Example: Question – How am I going to find someone to hire to design my website? Answer – By asking my friend who built his and hiring that person.)

_____

_____

_____

_____

If still not clear on what to do based on your answer(s) or if you feel you need additional actionable steps, continue asking yourself, *"HOW?"*

(Example: Question – How am I going to hire a person to design my website? Answer – By saving 1/4 of the total cost per week so I have all the money within a month.)

_____

_____

_____

_____

Keep asking yourself, *"HOW?"* until you identify clearly defined ACTIONABLE answers.

Record the ACTION STEPS you identified on the lines below.

_____

_____

_____

_____

_____

_____

_____

Find Your Motivating Desire in Business (Why?)

When finding your motivating desire, be sure your justification is honest and authentic. With this, it's perfectly appropriate to give yourself permission to be extremely self-centered because your motivation is what will give you the fuel you need to change. The answers to your reasoning of, *"Why?"* are crucial to your transformation.

62

Ask yourself "WHY?" Why do you want to achieve
_____?

(Example: Question – Why do I want to create a website? Answer – To have a place online to feature my information and products.)

_____

_____

_____

_____

Now, ask yourself, "*WHY?*" again and record your response.

(Example: Question – Why do I want to feature my information and products? Answer – So I can help others to solve their problems.)

_____

_____

_____

_____

Ask yourself "WHY?" a third time and record your response.

(Example: Question – Why do I want to help people to solve their problems? Answer – Because I feel like I'm here to educate others on the power of herbs.)

_____

_____

_____

_____

Review the responses to your *"WHY?"* questions above and summarize them in a statement that makes sense to you. Record your statement on the lines below.
(Example: I'm creating my website to serve as a platform to educate humanity about herbs.)

_____

_____

_____

_____

Lifetime Achievement Award Exercise

Complete the visualization activity below to get your engine revving with ideas to develop your *Now Purpose* in business.

Visualization

Envision yourself in the future. You've had a very successful career and you are being recognized by a panel of your peers. Because you have accomplished many of your goals in business, you have been nominated to receive a Lifetime Achievement Award for an aspect of business that *you* deem worthy of being rewarded for in your life.

Now imagine that you've just found out that *YOU* are the winner of the Lifetime Achievement Award! You're so excited, but realize that you have to write an acceptance speech for the awards ceremony. You sit down to begin writing. As you reflect on your long and successful career, consider what achievement and success mean for *you*.

Answer all of the questions below to create an acceptance speech based on all of your contributions and accomplishments in business. Be sure to include each of your answers in your acceptance speech.

- Who do you want to thank?
- Who did you help or serve?
- Who helped you?
- What did you accomplish or achieve?
- What impact did you have?
- What was a pivotal moment in your career?
- What have you accomplished that you are most proud of?

Write your acceptance speech on the lines below.

_____
_____
_____
_____
_____
_____
_____
_____
_____
_____
_____
_____
_____

NOW PURPOSE IN PERSONAL DEVELOPMENT

Personal development is the practice of improving one's abilities, talents and potential in effort to increase one's quality of life. It is pretty self-explanatory. When you engage in the process of personal development, you are essentially choosing aspects of yourself in which you would like to see growth and seeking out the assistance and/or resources necessary to feel more satisfied with yourself and ultimately, your life. As you engage in activities with the intention of personal development, you will watch yourself grow and evolve in meaningful and enriching ways.

Since personal development deals with the self, it can mean something different for everyone. One may see personal growth from more of a religious or spiritual sense. Another may say it's about engaging in intellectual development such as reading books and taking classes while someone else may elect to develop themselves through holistic modalities like acupuncture or Pilates. As with all of the areas of life, establishing and maintaining keen self-awareness will steer you in the right direction regarding your personal development.

Because this is about YOU and YOUR *Now Purpose*, make sure to apply the concept of personal development to *your* lifestyle. *Why?* Because it's *personal!* That's why!

Awareness Questions for Personal Development

What do you like about your current personal development?
(Examples: Exploring a variety of strategies from different people, meditation practice, reading a book every month, keeping a diary, etc.)

_____

_____

_____

_____

What do you dislike?
(Examples: Not feeling like I have enough time for myself, feeling like I'm not growing, can't afford self-help classes, judgment from family and friends, etc.)

_____

_____

_____

_____

What fears do you have about your personal development?
(Examples: Not reaching my potential, lacking resources, the unknown, wasting time and money with something that's not a good fit for me, etc.)

_____

_____

_____

_____

What frustrates you about personal development?

(Examples: Feeling as if I'm growing then hitting a plateau, too much information out there, too many teachers, looking outside of myself for answers, etc.)

_____

_____

_____

_____

What about personal development brings you joy and happiness?
(Examples: Getting a new book in the mail, meeting new people at seminars, finding new information, buying new "toys" like crystals, etc.)

_____

_____

_____

_____

What do you want most out of your personal development?
(Examples: To maximize my potential, money and abundance, like-minded friends, higher emotional intelligence, etc.)

_____

_____

_____

_____

What are your strongest gifts, talents, abilities or personality traits?
(Examples: Giving, strong-minded, leadership abilities, communication skills, etc.)

_____

_____
_____
_____

What are your biggest challenges?
(Examples: Procrastinating, overthinking, nervous and anxious, lacking confidence, etc.)

_____
_____
_____
_____

What are some beliefs you have about yourself that may be true or not?
(Examples: I don't have any talents, I'm not on the right path, my work ethic is weak, I'll never meet my potential, etc.)

_____
_____
_____
_____

Take note of any items you may have mentioned more than once. It is likely, they will help with your Lights of Awareness.

Lights of Awareness in Personal Development

The more specific you are, the clearer your purpose will be. The key is to focus on actionable items or things that you can physically DO.

Green Lights

What are you currently doing for personal development that you know you should be doing MORE?
(Examples: Studying Astrology, practicing martial arts, having self-control, being productive, etc.)

_____

_____

_____

_____

Yellow Lights

What are you currently doing that YOU feel like you should SLOW DOWN or not do as much?
(Examples: Overanalyzing, reading more information and not applying it, being hard on myself, surfing social media, etc.)

_____

_____

_____

_____

Red Lights

What are you currently doing that YOU know you should STOP doing for your personal development?
(Examples: Stealing, smoking weed, paying for services and not using my membership benefits, watching television, etc.)

_____

70

_____

_____

_____

Black Lights

What do you feel like you SHOULD BE doing that you're currently *not* doing for personal development?
(Examples: Learning Spanish, joining a club, playing piano, reading about Neuro-Linguistic Programming, etc.)

_____

_____

_____

Identify Your Action Steps in Personal Development (How?)

Review what you have written above, then select one of your Lights. Which of your Lights feels heaviest on your heart?
(Example: Having self-control)

_____

_____

_____

_____

Ask yourself, "HOW?" How am I going to achieve
_____?
(Example: Question – How am I going to have more self-control? Answer – By limiting the amount of time I spend engaging in

unproductive activities like surfing the internet and social media.)

_____

_____

_____

_____

Now, ask yourself, "HOW?" again.
(Example: Question – How am I going to limit my unproductive activities? Answer – By allocating free time every day and scheduling it.)

_____

_____

_____

_____

If you still have no clear actionable answer(s), or if you desire additional steps, ask yourself, "HOW?" again.
(Example: Question – How am I going to allocate free time and schedule it? Answer – By dedicating a calendar on my phone for free time with alarms and reminders to reinforce focus.)

_____

_____

_____

_____

Keep asking yourself, "HOW?" until you get clear and precise ACTIONABLE answers.

Write down your ACTION STEPS.

_____

_____

_____

_____

_____

_____

_____

_____

Find Your Motivating Desire in Personal Development (Why?)

When finding your motivating desire, be sure your justification is honest and authentic. With this, it's perfectly appropriate to give yourself permission to be extremely self-centered because your motivation is what will give you the fuel you need to change. The answers to your reasoning of, _"Why?"_ are crucial to your transformation.

Ask yourself, "WHY?" Why do I want to achieve ____?
(Example: Question – Why do I want to have more self-control? Answer – To improve my productivity and self-mastery.)

_____

_____

_____

_____

Now, ask yourself, "WHY?" again.
(Example: Question – Why do I want to improve my productivity and self-mastery? Answer – Because I want to achieve my dreams and aspirations.)

_____

_____
_____
_____

Lastly, ask yourself, "WHY?" a third time.
(Example: Question — Why do I want to achieve my dreams and aspirations? Answer — Because I don't want to leave this world with regrets.)

_____
_____
_____
_____

Write down your, *"WHY?"* in a sentence that makes sense to you.
(Example: I practice self-control so I don't have regrets when I transition.)

_____
_____
_____
_____

Researching Research Exercise

The purpose of this exercise is to review what you've been researching. There's a very good chance you have researched information regarding ways to improve yourself. Consciously or subconsciously, you probably have been looking up things on the internet that relate to personal development.

S. ALI MYERS

Currently, there are over 66 million Google search results for the keywords, "personal development." Obviously, people are very interested in the topic and are searching for something to support them as they seek to achieve personal growth. More than likely, you are one of them.

Look at the history on your phone, laptop, tablet and/or desktop for the past 6 months. What personal development information have you been looking up?

_____

_____

_____

_____

Check your bookmarks and saved pages on your device. What types of websites have you saved? What kind of information is on these sites?

_____

_____

_____

_____

What books have you purchased in the past 6 months? Do any relate to personal development?

_____

_____

_____

_____

Have you bought any magazines in the past 6 months? If so, do any of them have information or articles related to personal development?

_____

_____

_____

_____

Take the time to research your research. Notice the common themes that you've been looking in to and begin to apply what you've learned to your life. This sort of self-examination will probably lead you to your *Now Purpose*.

NOW PURPOSE IN RELATIONSHIPS

Relationships are bonds or connections created between two or more people. These connections can exist among blood relatives as well as those who are unrelated to us. Relationships can vary in intensity from intimate to platonic, close friendships to mere acquaintances. Some relationships are inherited while others are chosen. Relationships with family members---parents, cousins, aunts, uncles, etc. are inherited while relationships with friends, significant others, colleagues, etc. are relationships that we choose to enter into. These bonds can extend to anyone who is in your life in a small or big role. Whether the relationships are intimate or platonic, rewarding or disastrous, it is important for us to learn how to navigate them effectively.

While familial relationships often play a significant role in our lives, for the purposes of this chapter, relationships are in reference to bonds with people who *do not* share our bloodline. However, ultimately, the way you choose to apply the tools in this chapter is completely up to you. Take the liberty to use *Now Purpose Manual* as you see fit to find your purpose today.

For most people, marriage is the apex of relationships. Though technically, your spouse could also be viewed as a family member, this relationship was one that you *chose* to enter into. If you are married or in a committed relationship, you will probably focus more on your connection with your significant other than with your friends. Your primary relationship may be with your husband/wife or boyfriend/girlfriend or if you're not in an intimate relationship, it could be with your best friend.

Relationships are as unique as the individuals in them. Consequently, they will be different for everyone. If this area of life is one you feel drawn to make more purposeful, remember to allow the flexibility necessary for it to fit into your lifestyle.

Awareness Questions for Relationships

What do you like about your current relationships?
(Examples: Feeling like I have good friends, intimate conversations, always having somebody to do something with, sex with my significant other, etc.)

_____

_____

_____

_____

What do you dislike?
(Examples: The few buddies who always ask to borrow money, dishonesty, my partner's schedule at work, my friend's wife who always has an attitude, etc.)

_____

_____

_____

_____

What fears do you have about relationships?

(Examples: That my partner will leave me, being fully vulnerable, getting stabbed in the back, never getting married, etc.)

_____

_____

_____

_____

What frustrates you about relationships?
(Examples: Getting to know people, my partner leaving the toilet seat up, being alone, my friend cutting me off when I speak, etc.)

_____

_____

_____

_____

What about your relationships brings you joy and happiness?
(Examples: Going to parties, anniversaries, seeing the same person every morning, getting flowers for no reason, etc.)

_____

_____

_____

_____

What do you want most out of your relationships?
(Examples: Unconditional love, a shoulder to cry on, honesty, trust,   etc.)

_____

_____

_____

_____

What are the strongest assets that you bring to your relationships?
(Examples: Honest, trustworthy, good communicator, great at giving advice, etc.)

_____

_____

_____

_____

What are your biggest challenges or weaknesses in relationships?
(Examples: Closed off at times, lacking empathy, infidelity, being too needy, etc.)

_____

_____

_____

_____

What are some beliefs or assumptions you have about relationships that may be true or false?
(Examples: If you're not married by age 30 you are worthless, you should not have sex before marriage, birds of a feather flock together, your friends should be there for you whenever you need them, etc.)

_____

_____

_____

_____

Take note of any items you mentioned multiple times. More than likely, they will help with your Lights of Awareness.

Lights of Awareness in Relationships

The more specific you are, the clearer your purpose will be. The key is to focus on actionable items or things you can physically DO.

Green Lights

What are you currently doing for your relationship(s) that you know you should be doing MORE?
(Examples: Saying "I love you," more weekend getaways, having more trust in my friends, catching up with old friends, etc.)

_____

_____

_____

_____

Yellow Lights

What are you currently doing that YOU feel like you should SLOW DOWN or not do as much?
(Examples: Cracking and joking on friends less, less out-of-town meetings to be home more, spending less time with buddies on Friday nights, questioning my partner about their whereabouts, etc.)

_____

_____

_____

_____

Red Lights

What are you currently doing that YOU know you should STOP doing in your relationship(s)?
(Examples: Cheating, complaining about not getting attention, stop canceling dates or outings, comparing friends, etc.)

_____

_____

_____

_____

Black Lights

What do you feel like you should START doing that you're currently not doing in your relationship(s)?
(Examples: Inviting a partner to poker night, making surprise visits, sending birthday cards to old friends, learning to dance salsa for the class reunion, etc.)

_____

_____

_____

_____

Identify Your Action Steps in Relationships (How?)

Review what you have written above, then select one of your Lights. Which of your Lights feels heaviest on your heart?
(Example: Stop cheating on my spouse.)

_____

_____

_____

_____

Ask yourself, "HOW?" How am I going to achieve
_____?

(Example: Question – How am I going to stop cheating? Answer – By making sure I do not start any relationships with the opposite sex that may lead to infidelity.)

_____

_____

_____

Now, ask yourself, "HOW?" again.

(Example: Question – How am I going to avoid starting relationships with the opposite sex? Answer – By making sure my free time is allocated for activities with my partner and/or friends.)

_____

_____

_____

If still no clear actionable answer(s) or for additional steps, ask yourself, "HOW?" again. *(Example: Question – How am I going to allocate time for my friends and partner? Answer – By scheduling events one week ahead to avoid last-minute decisions.)*

Keep asking yourself, "HOW?" until you get clear and precise ACTIONABLE answers.

Write down your ACTION STEPS.

_____

_____

_____

_____

_____

_____

_____

Find Your Motivating Desire in Relationships (Why?)

When finding your motivating desire, be sure your justification is honest and authentic. With this, it's perfectly appropriate to give yourself permission to be extremely self-centered because your motivation is what will give you the fuel you need to change. The answers to your reasoning of, *"Why?"* are crucial to your transformation.

Ask yourself, "WHY?" Why do I want to achieve _____?
(Example: Question – Why do I want to stop cheating on my spouse? Answer – I know it's not right.)

_____

_____

_____

_____

Now, ask yourself, "WHY?" again.
(Example: Question – Why is it not right? Answer – Because I would not want them cheating on me.)

_____

_____

_____

_____

Lastly, ask yourself, "WHY?" for the third time.
(Example: Question – Why do I not want my partner cheating on me? A – Because I remember my parents going through infidelity issues and I didn't like how it felt.)

_____

_____

_____

_____

Write down your, "WHY?" in a sentence that makes sense to you.
(Example: I am faithful to my partner because I want to break the cycle of infidelity in my family.)

_____

_____

_____

_____

Survey Says Exercise

Communication is one of the keys to making relationships work. You interact with those around you through words and actions. Our actions can communicate just as effectively as our words. Ever

85

heard the saying, *actions speak louder than words?* This is because we what we do and how we act *says* a lot about who we are.

The Survey Says exercise will force you to "listen" to others. The survey will put your friends in a position to express how they feel about you and the relationship. Most profitable companies issue surveys and feedback cards to their customers. The best people to tell you about *you* are those you serve and those that surround you. *Are you open for some truths?*

To complete this exercise, you will need to open a free account at surveymonkey.com.
You can create a customized survey on the site. The beautiful thing about it is that it allows the people taking your survey to do so anonymously. This will serve well for you to get some straight answers and feedback because they will know their identity is hidden.

Here's what you need to do:

Step #1 - Create a new survey on surveymonkey.com.

Step #2 – Create questions to gain greater awareness of your relationships. You can make multiple choice and/or single answer questions. To get you started, here are a few example Survey Says questions to choose from:

What is something you like about me? *(Select Single Textbox to let them enter an answer.)*

On a scale of 1 to 10, how would you rate the value of our friendship? 1 – Very low and 10 – Very high *(Select Slider and input 1 for the left side and 10 for the right side.)*

What is something I can do, if anything, to improve the quality of our relationship? *(Select Single Textbox to let them enter an answer.)*

Is there anything you would like to share with me? *(Select Single Textbox to let them enter an answer.)*

Step #3 – Click *Done* and save. Then, click *Next* to go to the page where you can share the survey.

Step #4 – Click on *"Get Web Link"* so that you can share the survey and allow your friends to answer anonymously.

Step #5 – Share the link with 3-10 of your friends and analyze the answers.

Step #6 – Pay close attention to the survey answers you receive that match any of your Lights of Awareness for Relationships.

NOW PURPOSE IN PHYSICAL HEALTH

The physical shell that is your body is the vehicle for your soul in this lifetime, and its wellness has a tremendous impact on your overall quality of life. It's difficult to focus on achieving *any* goal if you're distracted by physical discomfort, ailment or disease. Your well-being is a necessity and it is paramount to your success. Ask anyone who is successful and I bet that they will tell you that their health is one of the most important things to them. *Why?* Because without good health and vitality, there can *be* no wealth. No success. No purpose fulfilled. Period. Healthful living is a prerequisite to purposeful living.

Your physical health is all about your body. Being aware of this major part of who you are is key to living a more purposeful life. Your strengths, your talents, your struggles, your obstacles and your vision for your form all play a huge role in both your self-image and self-perception. Having a strong and healthy physical body allows you to maintain the energy necessary to effectively house your soul and ultimately fulfill a *Now Purpose* in physical health and any other area of life.

Awareness Questions for Physical Health

What do you like about your physical being?
(Examples: Having all my fingers, toes, arms and legs, still being able to play ball, the way I look in a suit, having all my hair, etc.)

_____

_____

_____

_____

What do you dislike?
(*Examples: Turning gray, gaining weight by the year, cancer cells, migraines, etc.*)

_____

_____

_____

_____

What fears you have about your physical health?
(*Examples: That I will not be able to take care of myself in the next 10 years or so, limitations at work based on physical health, genetic diseases, people seeing tattoos I chose when I was less mature, etc.*)

_____

_____

_____

_____

What frustrates you about your physical health?
(*Examples: Having to work-out to stay in shape, eating healthy, harder to lose weight as I get older, impotence, etc.*)

_____

_____

_____

_____

What do you desire most from your physical health?

(Examples: To complete a marathon, have regular blood pressure, convert to veganism, be a master yogi, etc.)

_____

_____

_____

_____

What are your strongest attributes for physical health?
(Examples: Endurance, work ethic, strong arms, strong teeth and bones, etc.)

_____

_____

_____

_____

What are your biggest physical challenges?
(Examples: Work too much to go to the gym, no work-out partner, overeating, insecure when naked, etc.)

_____

_____

_____

_____

What are some beliefs or assumptions you have about physical health that may be true or false?
(Examples: I'm not attractive, I need to lose 15 pounds, healthier people are skinny, veganism is the perfect dietary choice, etc.)

_____

_____

_____

_____

Take note of any items you mentioned multiple times. More than likely they will help with your Lights of Awareness.

Lights of Awareness in Physical Health

The more specific you are, the clearer your purpose will be. The key is to focus on actionable items or things you can physically DO.

Green Lights

What are you currently doing for your physical health that you know you should be doing MORE?
(Examples: Going to the gym more to workout, more veggies, meditate more, getting massages, etc.)

_____
_____
_____
_____

Yellow Lights

What are you currently doing that YOU feel like you should SLOW DOWN or not do as much?
(Examples: Drinking less beer, eating sugar, getting tattoos, going to sleep too late, etc.)

_____
_____
_____
_____

91

Red Lights

What are you currently doing that YOU know you should STOP doing for your physical health?
(Examples: Stop smoking cigarettes, no more red meat, stop

_____

_____

_____

_____

Black Lights

What do you feel like you should START doing that you're currently NOT DOING for your physical health?
(Examples: Start getting annual physical exams, begin a yoga practice, becoming vegan, start checking my blood pressure every 3 months, etc.)

_____

_____

_____

_____

Identify Your Action Steps in Physical Health (How?)

Review what you have written above, then select one of your Lights. Which of your Lights feels heaviest on your heart?
(Example: Becoming vegan)

_____

_____

_____

_____

Ask yourself, "HOW?" How are you going to achieve
_____?
(Example: Question – How am I going to become vegan?
Answer – By not eating meat or dairy products.)

_____

_____

_____

_____

Now, ask yourself, "HOW?" again.
(Example: Question – How am I going to stop eating meat and
dairy? Answer – By eating vegan-friendly foods, especially fruits
and vegetables.)

_____

_____

_____

_____

If still no clear actionable answer(s), or for additional
steps, ask yourself, "HOW?" again. *(Example: Question –*
How am I going to eat more vegan foods? Answer – By
purchasing a few vegan cookbooks and preparing meals daily.)

Keep asking yourself, "HOW?" until you get clear and
precise ACTIONABLE answers.

Write down your ACTION STEPS.

_____

_____

_____

_____

_____

_____

_____

_____

Find Your Motivating Desire in Physical Health (Why?)

When finding your motivating desire, be sure your justification is honest and authentic. With this, it's perfectly appropriate to give yourself permission to be extremely self-centered because your motivation is what will give you the fuel you need to change. The answers to your reasoning of, _"Why?"_ are crucial to your transformation.

Ask yourself, "WHY?" Why do I want to achieve _____?
(Example: Question – Why do I want to become vegan? Answer – I feel like it will give me way more energy.)

_____

_____

_____

_____

Now, ask yourself, "WHY?" again.
(Example: Question – Why do I want to more energy? Answer – Because I want to feel like I did when I was in my twenties.)

_____

_____

_____

_____

Lastly, ask yourself, "WHY?" a third time.
(Example: Question – Why do I want to feel like I'm in my twenties again? Answer – Because that's when I felt most alive.)

_____

_____

_____

Write down your "WHY?" in a sentence that makes sense to you.
(Example: I practice veganism to feel alive as if I was 20 years old.)

_____

_____

_____

Mirrors Speak Exercise

Mirrors are powerful devices. Some consider them to be portals or gateways to other dimensions. Regardless, there is something fascinating about mirrors. There also seems to be something mysterious about them.

The main thing a mirror does is reflect. Any physical object in its view will be reflected back. This exercise will force you to reflect on yourself. Try to go beyond the physical as you gain greater awareness of your body and your health.

For this exercise, all you need is a mirror, preferably full-length.

First, look at yourself in the mirror for a minimum of 2 minutes. You may choose to do this nude if you like.

After 2 minutes of reflecting on your physical health, answer the following questions and use each answer to guide changes in your behavior that will result in enhancing your physical health and self-image.

What do I like about the way I look?

_____
_____
_____
_____

What do I dislike about the way I look?

_____
_____
_____
_____

What must I accept because I can't change it?

_____
_____
_____
_____

S. ALI MYERS

What can I work to improve?

_____
_____
_____
_____

How do I feel physically?

_____
_____
_____
_____

What is my body telling me it wants the most?

_____
_____
_____
_____

NOW PURPOSE IN MENTAL HEALTH

Your mental health is the condition of your psychological and emotional well-being. If physical health relates to the external or body, then mental health relates to the internal or the mind. While very different, it is important to note that the two are interrelated. The mind affects the body and vice versa. For example, ingesting an unhealthy diet can lead to digestive imbalances which result in fatigue and symptoms of anxiety and depression. Conversely, persistent worry or stressful thinking can lead to increased cortisol levels in the body causing weight gain, greying hair or hair loss, somatic pain, etc. Based on this, if we do not monitor our thinking and minimize our stress, it can have an adverse impact on our overall health. In essence, the quality of our lives is contingent upon the quality of our thoughts.

The state of our mental health is directly related to the quality of our thoughts. Thoughts are incessant. They first arise in our minds, and then they are filtered outward via our emotional responses. We *"hear"* our thoughts, but we *feel* our emotions. Once again, this is all an internal process that is ultimately demonstrated physically. *Why?* Because thoughts are things. We are what we think. The things that we think about often will eventually show up in our physical experience.

Gaining awareness in the mental and emotional health area of life may be one of the more challenging to ensure. We tend to be overly biased or heavily judgmental of ourselves. Making an honest and unbiased assessment of the status of your mental health is critical for you to learn how to control your inner world and move toward fulfilling a *Now Purpose* in this particular area of life.

Awareness Questions for Mental Health

What do you like about your current mental state?
(Examples: Being comfortable in my own skin, feeling smart, having empathy, usually happy and upbeat, etc.)

What do you dislike?
(Examples: Lacking confidence, feeling weak, feeling sorry for myself, still grieving over my lost loved one, etc.)

What are your fears?
(Examples: Public speaking, spiders, heights, driving on the highway, etc.)

_____
_____
_____

What are your frustrations at the moment?
(Examples: Going to work every day, insensitive people, not knowing my purpose, traffic jams on the way to work, etc.)

_____
_____
_____
_____

What makes you angry?
(Examples: Wars, cheating, lies, people making fun of others, etc.)

_____
_____
_____
_____

What brings you the most joy and happiness?
(Examples: Getting paid, spirituality and metaphysics, partying, singing, etc.)

_____
_____
_____
_____

What do you desire most right now?
(Examples: Sexual pleasure, to learn how to meditate, more money, a stronger bond with my parents, etc.)

_____
_____
_____
_____

What are your strongest innate abilities?
(Examples: Creativity, ambition, passion, multi-talented, etc.)

_____
_____
_____
_____

What are your biggest emotional struggles?
(Examples: Arrogance, lacking confidence, depression, suicidal thoughts, etc.)

_____
_____
_____
_____

How do you feel right now?
(Examples: Content, bored, horny, happy, etc.   )

_____
_____
_____
_____

Take note of any items that you mentioned multiple times. More than likely, they will help with your Lights of Awareness.

Lights of Awareness in Mental Health

The more specific you are, the clearer your purpose will be. The key is to focus on identifying actionable items or things you can physically DO.

Green Lights

What are you currently doing for your mental well-being that you know you should do MORE of?
(Examples: Meditating more, showing gratitude, channeling my anger, being more confident, etc.)

_____

_____

_____

_____

Yellow Lights

What are you currently doing that YOU feel like you should SLOW DOWN or not do as much?
(Examples: Crying less, limiting self-criticism, thinking too much, always taking the easy way out, etc.)

_____

_____

_____

_____

Red Lights

What are you currently doing that YOU know you should STOP doing for your mental well-being?

(Examples: Stop self-sabotage, stop having insecurities, an addictive habit, not sharing my inner-most thoughts with my partner, etc.)

_____

_____

_____

_____

Black Lights

What do you feel like you SHOULD BE doing that you're currently *not* doing for your mental well-being?
(Examples: Starting a diary to record my inner thoughts, positive affirmations, beginning a gratitude journal, sharing my songs with the world, etc.)

_____

_____

_____

_____

Identify Your Action Steps in Mental Health (How?)

Review what you have written above, then select one of your Lights. Which of your Lights feels heaviest on your heart?
(Example: Sharing my songs with the world.)

_____

_____

_____

_____

Ask yourself, "HOW?" How am I going to achieve ____?

103

(Example: Question – How am I going to share my songs with the world? Answer – By starting a YouTube channel to feature my work.)

_____

_____

_____

_____

Now, ask yourself, "HOW?" again.
(Example: Question – How am I going to start a YouTube channel? A – By researching YouTube for the best tips.)

_____

_____

_____

_____

If you still have no clear actionable answer(s), or if you'd like additional steps, ask yourself, "HOW?" again. *(Example: Question – How am I going to research YouTube for tips on starting a channel? Answer – By searching "YouTube channel tips" in the search engine and taking notes from the top 5.)*

Continue to ask yourself, "HOW?" until you get clear, precise and ACTIONABLE answers.

Write down your ACTION STEPS.

_____

_____

_____

_____

_____

_____

_____

_____

Find Your Motivating Desire in Mental Health (Why?)

When finding your motivating desire, be sure your justification is honest and authentic. With this, it's perfectly appropriate to give yourself permission to be extremely self-centered because your motivation is what will give you the fuel you need to change. The answers to your reasoning of, *"Why?"* are crucial to your transformation.

Ask yourself, "WHY?" Why do I want to achieve _____?
(Example: Question – Why do I want to share my songs with the world? Answer – I believe my songs come to me so I can share them with others.)

_____

_____

_____

_____

Now, ask yourself, "WHY?" again.
(Example: Question – Why do I believe my songs come to me for sharing purposes? Answer – The first person I shared a song with told me they needed to hear the message because they were dealing with depression.)

_____

_____

_____

_____

Lastly, ask yourself, "WHY?" for the third time.
(Example: Question – Why did that person need to hear the message in my song? Answer – Because they asked the Spirit to help them to move beyond their depression.)

_____

_____

_____

_____

Summarize your *"WHY?"* in a sentence that makes sense to you and write it on the lines below.
(Example: I share my songs with the world because Spirit guides people to my music when they need it the most.)

_____

_____

_____

_____

Express Yourself Exercise

Human beings normally express themselves based on their current feelings. In any given moment, emotions can change or shift in any direction, causing self-expression to be a vehicle of variance that the world must interpret to gain a greater understanding of us, our desires and our needs. In order to be understood clearly, it's important to routinely conduct a self-inventory of your emotions. This is most imperative if you find yourself in a somber or depressed state. Recognizing your emotions and transmuting them is a habit that takes practice to master.

This exercise will help you acknowledge your emotional state on a conscious level. Since awareness is the first step to purpose, it is necessary for you to become more aware so that you can be purposeful with your emotions. Making this a practice will help you to know how to express yourself far more effectively.

For the Express Yourself exercise, take your first, middle and/or last name. Then, choose an adjective, emotion or word that best describes how you feel right now for each letter.

Example: A L I
I feel...
A – Appreciated
L – Loved
I – Insane

Next, choose the emotion that is strongest. What can you do with it? What can you do about it?

_____
_____
_____
_____

You can do this exercise as often as you'd like to get a quick inventory on your emotions. You may also use general words instead of your name to add more variety.

NOW PURPOSE IN FAMILY

In most societies across the globe, the family unit serves as the foundational construct to individuals' social development. From communication and caring for ourselves and others to shaping our morals, core values and beliefs, the family unit is the primary source for learning.

A family is generally considered a group of people related by blood, but adoptees, spouses and in-laws can also be considered integral parts of a family unit. Unlike friends and significant others, you don't *choose* your family. You are either born into a family or you start your own when you have children.

The commonality between family and friends is that we choose who we have closer bonds with. Most people have several relatives --- siblings, cousins, aunts, uncles, nephews, nieces and maybe even grandchildren. Among those, it is likely that you naturally gravitate toward specific relative(s) more than others. Therefore, you *do* choose who you have a stronger bond with. The closeness of these bonds is not limited to physical proximity. Even if you don't live near each other, you may have a stronger relationship with a family member who lives farther away than with one who lives just down the street.

Having a *Now Purpose* in family suggests that you realize that you would like to build upon some of your familial relationships. Developing this area of life may require

S. ALI MYERS

patience and tolerance, but your diligence is sure to result in the fulfillment of lasting ties with those you love the most.

Awareness Questions for Family

What do you like about your family?
(Examples: We get along for the most part, big family, having a famous cousin, family reunions, etc.)

_____

_____

_____

_____

What do you dislike?
(Examples: Not seeing my grandmother as much, how far my mom lives from me, my alcoholic uncle ruining parties, that I can't have kids, etc.)

_____

_____

_____

_____

What fears do you have about your family?
(Examples: That my brother won't graduate, my mother not being alive to see me live my purpose, getting divorced, losing my health insurance, etc.)

_____

_____

_____

_____

What frustrates you about your family?
(Examples: My aunt never bringing a dish for the reunions, everyone not showing up for festivities, my sister's boyfriend cheating on her, some of my family's obscene social media pages, etc.)

_____
_____
_____
_____

What about your family brings you joy and happiness?
(Examples: Family reunions, someone having a baby, baby showers, quiet evenings by the fireplace, etc.)

_____
_____
_____
_____

What do you want most from your family?
(Examples: Support, communication, trust, honesty, etc.)

_____
_____
_____
_____

What qualities or abilities do you have that can help your family?
(Examples: Cooking and grilling out, a big house to gather family, always helping out as needed, providing for my family, etc.)

_____

_____

_____

_____

What are your biggest challenges?
(Examples: Flirting with other women even though I'm married, don't call my mom as much as I should, haven't spoken with my brother in 15 years, hard to let go of the past, etc.)

_____

_____

_____

What are some beliefs or assumptions you have about family that may be true or false?
(Examples: Family should look out for each other, blood over water, love should be unconditional, you shouldn't marry outside of your race, etc.)

_____

_____

_____

_____

Take note of any items you mentioned multiple times. More than likely, they will help with your Lights of Awareness.

Lights of Awareness in Family

The more specific you are, the clearer your purpose will be. The key is to focus on actionable items or things you can physically DO.

Green Lights

What are you currently doing for your family that you know you should do MORE of?
(Examples: Calling my mom more, letting go of the past, visiting my aunt's grave, teaching my nephew about girls and dating, etc.)

_____

_____

_____

_____

Yellow Lights

What are you currently doing that YOU feel like you should SLOW DOWN or not do as much?
(Examples: Spoiling my niece, choosing Florida over California for the family reunions, posting my somewhat offensive Facebook posts, working too much and not spending that time with my family,   *etc.)*

_____

_____

_____

_____

Red Lights

What are you currently doing that YOU know you should STOP doing for your family?
(Examples: Cursing around the little ones, being drunk at reunions, being mentally abusive, smoking around the little ones, etc.)

_____

_____

_____

_____

Black Lights

What do you feel like you SHOULD BE doing that
you're not currently doing for your family?
(*Examples: Writing my cousin in jail, visiting my great-aunt,
spending time with my younger brother, calling to voice my opinion,
etc.*)

_____

_____

_____

_____

Identify Your Action Steps in Family (How?)

Review what you have written above, then select one of
your Lights. Which of your Lights feels heaviest on
your heart?
(*Example: Spending time with my younger brother.*)

_____

_____

_____

_____

Ask yourself, "HOW?" How am I going to achieve
_____?

NOW PURPOSE IN FAMILY

(Example: Question – How am I going to spend time with my brother? Answer – By calling him and seeing what he's into nowadays.)

_____

_____

_____

_____

Now, ask yourself, "HOW?" again.
(Example: Question – How am I going to call him? I don't have his number. Answer – By contacting everyone in the family to see if they have his number.)

_____

_____

_____

_____

If still no clear actionable answer(s) or for additional steps, ask yourself, "HOW?" again. *(Example: Question – How am I going to contact everyone in the family? Answer – By calling or texting at least one family member per day until I get his number.)*

_____

_____

_____

_____

Keep asking yourself, "HOW?" until you get clear and precise ACTIONABLE answers.

Write down your ACTION STEPS.

_____
_____
_____
_____
_____
_____
_____

Find Your Motivating Desire in Family (Why?)

When finding your motivating desire, be sure your justification is honest and authentic. With this, it's perfectly appropriate to give yourself permission to be extremely self-centered because your motivation is what will give you the fuel you need to change. The answers to your reasoning of, *"Why?"* are crucial to your transformation.

Ask yourself, "WHY?" Why do I want to achieve ____?
(Example: Question – Why do I want to spend more time with my brother? Answer – I feel like I owe him something.)

_____
_____
_____
_____

Now, ask yourself, "WHY?" again.
(Example: Question – Why do I feel like I owe him something? Answer – Because I have not been there for him when he's reached out to me.)

_____

Lastly, ask yourself, "WHY?" for the third time.
(Example: Question – Why have I not been there for him? Answer – Because I didn't want him to be around me back in the day because I was miserable.)

Write down your "WHY?" in a sentence that makes sense to you.
(Example: I spend time with my brother to show him that I'm not the same person I used to be.)

Family Ties Exercise

Family is a very broad and blanketed term that describes a connection with others in the same bloodline. Depending on the size of your family, you will have few or many people that share this bond with you. However, we still choose who we want to have deeper relationships with.

When pursuing a *Now Purpose* in the family area of life, you will more than likely have a select list of people in mind that you wish to strengthen relationships with. It would be naive to think that you will actively have a relationship with *every* member of your family. Yes, you may socialize together when you attend family functions, but to consistently keep up with *everyone* may prove to be quite challenging to say the least.

The Family Ties exercise will help you find commonalities with select family members. These ties will serve as common grounds from which you may elect to build a relationship or identify things to do related to your common interests.

First, write down a few people in your family that you want to have a closer bond with.

_____

_____

_____

_____

Ask each of them what their favorite things to do are.

_____

_____

_____

_____

Ask them where their favorite places to go are.

_____

_____

_____

_____

What are their favorite movie genres?

_____

_____

_____

_____

What's their favorite type of food?

_____

_____

_____

_____

What places do they want to travel to?

_____

_____

_____

_____

From the list you collect, highlight or mark common interests that you share. These ties will serve as a list of things to do with that particular family member and a positive starting point for strengthening your bond.

NOW PURPOSE IN LEISURE & FUN

Life without fun. Difficult to imagine? It *should* be, but more and more, people are trading their hobbies and more authentic interests for the pursuit of material gain. Days inundated with checking e-mails, business meetings, household responsibilities and striving to cross items off of to-do lists have replaced more traditional leisurely activities in the millennium. Today's leisure has been reduced to surfing the web and scrolling through various social media sites. It's no wonder that now, more than ever, people are feeling called to pursue more purposeful lives.

Over time, choosing not to prioritize your pleasures, will lead to lackluster living, boredom and dissatisfaction. Leisure and fun, or entertainment, is a very important area of life. In fact, it's essential. While material pursuits are important, striking a balance between work and play carries even more weight. Recalling and involving ourselves in what brings us joy is necessary to live a life that we love.

Exploring this *Now Purpose* will not only be fun, it will give us a glimpse into our inner child. Much can be learned from our youth. Children have fun *all day*! It is adults who need to give themselves permission to let loose sometimes!

Leisure time can be rewarding when spent alone or with others. Some like to have fun in groups while others

119

prefer their own company. As with every area of life, it will be different for each individual. Focus on yourself and what *you* want to do, but don't forget...have *FUN!*

Awareness Questions for Leisure & Fun

What do you like to do for fun?
(Examples: Traveling, reading books, watching television, dining out at new restaurants, etc.)

_____

_____

_____

_____

What are your *least* favorite things to do for fun?
(Examples: Going to the movies, sporting events, playing video games, card games, etc.)

_____

_____

_____

_____

What fears do you have about leisure and fun?
(Examples: It takes money to have fun, spending too much time to do something that doesn't pay the bills, not being able to do what I want to do, not having enough time to enjoy myself, etc.)

_____

_____

_____

_____

What frustrates you about leisure and fun?

S. ALI MYERS

(Examples: Friends' busy work schedules, limited places to eat in my city, watched all the new shows on Netflix, it takes money to have fun, etc.)

_____

_____

_____

_____

What would you do all day if you didn't have to work or take care of responsibilities?
(Examples: Read books, write, sing songs, go shopping, etc.)

_____

_____

_____

_____

What were your favorite things to do as a child?
(Examples: Color, draw, play musical instruments, sing in the mirror, etc.)

_____

_____

_____

_____

What were your *least* favorite things to do as a child?
(Examples: Clean my room, brush my teeth, go to church, take baths with my brother, etc.)

_____

_____

_____

_____

Who do you know, personally or not, that appears to have a fun life?
(Examples: My brother, best friend, etc.)

_____

_____

_____

_____

What does the person do that you think is fun and entertaining?
(Examples: Goes clubbing, has many friends, travels often, lives in the country, etc.)

_____

_____

_____

_____

Take note of any items you mentioned multiple times. More than likely, they will help with your Lights of Awareness.

Lights of Awareness in Leisure & Fun

The more specific you are, the clearer your purpose will be. The key is to focus on actionable items or things you can physically DO.

S. ALI MYERS

Green Lights

What are you currently doing for fun and leisure that you *know* you should do MORE of?
(Examples: Reading books, traveling more, eating out more, playing basketball, etc.)

Yellow Lights

What are you currently doing that YOU feel like you should SLOW DOWN or not do as much?
(Examples: Work less, spending less money on groceries to eat out more, staying in the house on Saturdays, helping family move in and out of houses, etc.)

Red Lights

What are you currently doing that YOU know you should STOP doing for more fun and entertainment?
(Examples: Stop prolonging my vacation, stop buying expensive shoes, stop working on the weekends, etc.)

_____
_____
_____

Black Lights

What do you feel like you SHOULD START doing that you're currently not doing for fun and leisure?
(Examples: Start traveling to Africa, start a travel account to save money, reading one book every week, start taking part in the annual basketball game at work, etc.)

Identify Your Action Steps in Leisure & Fun (How?)

Review what you have written above, then select one of your Lights. Which of your Lights feels heaviest on your heart?
(Example: Playing more basketball.)

_____
_____
_____
_____

Ask yourself, "HOW?" How am I going to achieve _____?
(Example: Question – How am I going to play more basketball? Answer – By starting a league for amateurs.)

_____
_____
_____
_____

Now, ask yourself, "HOW?" again.
(Example: Question – How am I going to start a league for amateurs? Answer – By promoting it throughout the city.)

_____

_____

_____

_____

If still no clear actionable answer(s) or for additional steps, ask yourself, "HOW?" again. *(Example: Question – How am I going to promote my league throughout the city? Answer – By printing out fliers and hiring some teenagers to pass them out door-to-door and on cars in parking lots.)*

_____

_____

_____

Keep asking yourself, "HOW?" until you get clear and precise ACTIONABLE answers.

Write down your ACTION STEPS.

_____

_____

_____

_____

_____

_____

_____

Find Your Motivating Desire in Leisure & Fun (Why?)

When finding your motivating desire, be sure your justification is honest and authentic. With this, it's perfectly appropriate to give yourself permission to be extremely self-centered because your motivation is what will give you the fuel you need to change. The answers to your reasoning of, *"Why?"* are crucial to your transformation.

Ask yourself, "WHY?" Why do you want to achieve _____?
(Example: Question – Why do I want to play more basketball? Answer – So that I can feel young again.)

_____

_____

_____

_____

Now, ask yourself, "WHY?" again.
(Example: Question – Why do I want to feel young again? Answer – Because I know I don't have too many more active years.)

_____

_____

_____

_____

Lastly, ask yourself, "WHY?" for the third time.

(Example: Question – Why do I not have too many more active years? Answer – Because I'm feeling drained by work and my body is falling apart.)

Write down your "WHY?" in a sentence that makes sense to you.
(Example: I play basketball to reverse the feeling of being drained and physically unfit.)

_____

_____

_____

_____

Fun Facts Exercise

For some people, it's difficult to have fun, especially if they wear the badge of "all work and no play." The Fun Facts exercise will help you discover more ways to have fun by taking an analytical approach.

In order to do this exercise, you will state facts about yourself. The objective is for you to base your answers solely on your personal experience. You will not have to make up anything or exercise any creativity. Heck, you may even have a little fun!

Answer each question to the best of your ability. Some facts may be harder to recall than others. Have fun!

What are the last three things you've done for fun and entertainment, big or small, with others or alone?

_____

_____

_____

_____

What were ALL of your hobbies as a kid?

_____

_____

_____

_____

Look up the definition of *fun*. What have you done in the past month that fits the definition?

_____

_____

_____

_____

Look up the definition of *leisure*. What have you done in the past month that fits the definition?

_____

_____

_____

_____

If you have a job or run a business, what did you do on your last day off?

_____

_____

_____

_____

The phone rings. It's your doctor and she has bad news for you. She tells you that you have a rare disease that's incurable. You're the first person to be diagnosed with it. You must only do fun things or you're going to die. What are you going to do?

_____

_____

_____

_____

Hopefully, you have listed some things that you deem fun and entertaining. Joy is a gift of life. Do everything that you can to find it!

NOW PURPOSE IN FINANCES

Earth is a physical and material world. In this earthly reality, our material needs must get met in order for us to feel that we are experiencing a comfortable existence. In order for our material needs to get met, the proper resources need to be accessible to us. *And, what is this resource that we need?* Money. While there are many things that come to us for free---love, friendship, joy and the like---ultimately, there are still many things needed that will require money.

Finances and money are important for material success. We all have something we want to do or get when we have more money. Even if you *are* materially successful, you still have a responsibility to ensure your financial security. All financial situations may be different, but in order for them to grow, a good deal of careful planning and direction is required.

If you are drawn to make your finances more purposeful, I'm assuming you want more of it or to do something beneficial with what you already have. The key to finding purpose for your money is to identify a meaningful use for it. Having money is one thing. *Doing* something purposeful with it is another.

Awareness Questions for Finances

What do you like about your current financial situation?

(Examples: Receiving money weekly via paycheck, my career, bonuses at work, I'm saving money every month, etc.)

_____

_____

_____

_____

What do you dislike?

(Examples: Working many hours to get a good pay check, my work schedule, not having enough money to invest in real estate, taxes, etc.)

_____

_____

_____

_____

What fears do you have about money?

(Examples: That I'm not going to have enough to retire, inflation, that the market will crash, getting robbed, etc.)

_____

_____

_____

_____

What frustrates you about money?

(Examples: Money is not real because it's not backed by gold, taxes, expensive insurance, trading time for money, etc.)

_____

_____

_____

_____

What about your finances brings you joy and happiness?
(Examples: Cashing my check, getting big bonuses, finding money on the street, saving for retirement, etc.)

_____

_____

_____

_____

How do you currently make money?
(Examples: Paycheck from work, small lottery winnings, investments, etc.)

_____

_____

_____

_____

What investments or assets do you have (things that are worth money or valuable)?
(Examples: Jewelry, gold, coins, vending machines, etc.)

_____

_____

_____

_____

What can money *not* do for you?
(Examples: Buy me love, make me feel like I'm doing something with my life, make me more attractive, fix my broken heart, etc.)

_____

_____

_____

_____

What are your biggest financial strengths?
(Examples: Saving money, budgeting, researching things to invest in, attract money easily, etc.)

_____

_____

_____

_____

What are your biggest challenges with money?
(Examples: Actually investing it in something, diversifying my portfolio, trusting advisors, saying no to family asking to borrow money, etc.)

_____

_____

_____

_____

What are some beliefs or assumptions you have about finances and money that may be true or false?
(Examples: All problems go away when you reach a high income bracket, money is the root of all evil, rich people are snobs, giving away your money is the best thing you can do, etc.)

_____

_____

_____

_____

Take note of any items you mentioned multiple times. More than likely, they will help with your Lights of Awareness.

Lights of Awareness in Finances

The more specific you are, the clearer your purpose will be. The key is to focus on actionable items or things you can physically DO.

Green Lights

What are you currently doing for your finances that you know you should do MORE of?
(Examples: Investing more, saving money, getting more bonuses, researching investments, etc.)

_____

_____

_____

_____

Yellow Lights

What are you currently doing that YOU feel like you should SLOW DOWN or not do as much?
(Examples: Spending money on clothes, scrolling on Facebook less to research investments more, trading time for money, vacationing less, etc.)

_____

_____

_____

_____

S. ALI MYERS

Red Lights

What are you currently doing that YOU know you should STOP doing for your financial situation?
(Examples: Buying cigarettes, stop doubting my entrepreneurial mind, stop comparing my money to others', stop delaying my real estate investments, etc.)

_____

_____

_____

_____

Black Lights

What do you feel like you SHOULD START doing that you're currently *not* doing with regard to finances and money?
(Examples: Start investing in multi-unit homes, get a mentor, attend investment conferences, go to local meet-ups for business professionals, etc.)

_____

_____

_____

_____

Identify Your Action Steps in Finances (How?)

Review what you have written above, then select one of your Lights. Which of your Lights feels heaviest on your heart?
(Example: Saving more money.)

_____

_____
_____
_____

Ask yourself, "HOW?" How am I going to achieve _____?
(Example: Question – How am I going to save more money?
Answer – By increasing the percentage I save from my paychecks.)

_____
_____
_____
_____

Now, ask yourself, "HOW?" again.
(Example: Question – How am I going to increase the saving
percentage? Answer – By saving 15% of my paycheck instead of
10%.)

_____
_____
_____
_____

If still no clear actionable answer(s) or for additional
steps, ask yourself, "HOW?" again. *(Example: Question –*
How am I going to save 15% of my paycheck? Answer – By
contacting my bank and setting up an automatic savings account.)

_____
_____
_____
_____

Keep asking yourself, "HOW?" until you get clear and
precise ACTIONABLE answers.

Write down your ACTION STEPS.

_____

_____

_____

_____

_____

_____

_____

_____

Find Your Motivating Desire in Finances (Why?)

When finding your motivating desire, be sure your justification is honest and authentic. With this, it's perfectly appropriate to give yourself permission to be extremely self-centered because your motivation is what will give you the fuel you need to change. The answers to your reasoning of, _"Why?"_ are crucial to your transformation.

Ask yourself, "WHY?" Why do I want to achieve _____?
(Example: Question – Why do I want to save more money? Answer – To have more funds for investments.)

_____

_____

_____

_____

Now, ask yourself, "WHY?" again.

(Example: Question – Why do I want more investment funds? Answer – Because I want to purchase a multi-unit apartment to rent out.)

_____

_____

_____

_____

Lastly, ask yourself, "WHY?" for the third time.
(Example: Question – Why do I want to invest in a multi-unit building? Answer – Because I know it will pay for all my retirement expenses and travels.)

_____

_____

_____

_____

Write down your, "WHY?" in a sentence that makes sense to you.
(Example: I save 15% of my money to invest in real estate for my retirement and travel.)

_____

_____

_____

_____

Instant Millionaire Exercise

As a child or young adult, did you ever play the game, *What Would You Do with a Million Dollars?* I bet you did! Hell, you may *still* play it! I remember sitting around with my buddies talking about what we were going to do when we "blow up" and get rich. There were absolutely *no* limits either!

Do your best to get in a zone where you know you have *millions* of dollars! You can sit for a few minutes and imagine or visualize money *pouring* into your accounts! See the money growing. *Own it.* It's *yours* and you deserve every single penny!

After you *really* feel like you have at least a million bucks, answer the following questions.

How did you get your million dollars?

_____
_____
_____
_____

What skills and resources did you use to get your millions?

_____
_____
_____
_____

What do you want to invest in now that you have all this money?

_____
_____
_____
_____

What do you want to buy?

_____

_____

_____

_____

What is your ultimate goal or long-term plan for your millions?

_____

_____

_____

_____

UNIVERSAL PURPOSES

There are some common life purpose traits that everyone shares. Through personal experience and my professional work with thousands of people all over the world, I've noticed a pattern involving these traits within people from varying walks of life. I call these traits *universal purposes*. Universal purposes reveal the life template intrinsic to humanity. These aspects of the human life template are experienced by everyone. They will inevitably show up in your life as well as others'.

There are three core universal purposes. Let these universal purposes be part of your internal navigation system. Allow them to help you reach your *Now Purpose* along with your spiritual guidance, which you will learn about in the next chapter. Notice how the universal purposes were always present in your life and observe how they reveal themselves in the future. Maintaining a conscious understanding of these purposes will assist mankind in attaining godhood.

Growth and Evolution

Many ancient cultures, including Kemetic (Egyptian), Eastern Indian and Native American civilizations, viewed Earth as a place for man to master himself or to evolve. The ancients had a name for this evolution. They called it Enlightenment. The process of incarnating over and over again is a system to perfect the soul. The soul uses the human form to master certain lessons and evolve back into the Source or Creator

(Universe, God, Primordium, etc.). This growth process is necessary to reach Enlightenment. Even if you don't believe in Enlightenment, would you agree that people, for the most part, have a desire to better themselves? Regardless of people's actions, the core desire of humanity is to do and be better.

The best example of human growth is demonstrated during childhood. Children have dreams of growing up and becoming a doctor, firefighter, pilot, etc. As children, we look forward to growing up and learning to drive, go to college and get married. There's something inside every child that forces them to look ahead or GROW and EVOLVE. What they choose to grow and evolve into is as unique to each individual as a fingerprint.

There's a force within each of us that calls for growth and evolution. The simple act of waking up each morning and going about your day is a mundane example of growth. No matter how well you do each day, there's always a little voice in your head urging you to do better. Many ignore this voice, but they can't deny its existence.

We learn something new every day. It may not be something significant. More than likely, it's so small that you don't even notice it. However, if you were to go about your day consciously, observing the details of each moment, you would notice something new is happening all the time. We've been conditioned not to notice or value subtle changes and occurrences.

142

In science, there's a term, *neuroplasticity*, which describes how the brain changes based on learning. These brain patterns are constantly changing and evolving as we grow in age. This biological process is evidence of our incessant evolution.

Most everyone can see that growth and evolution is a normal part of life. It occurs on a daily basis practically everywhere we look. No matter your religious or spiritual background, it is apparent. The fact that you are reading this book is proof that you too are aware of its existence!

Sharing Your Gifts, Talents and Abilities

Another universal purpose for humanity is to share gifts. Don't think you have any gifts or talents? I'm sure you can think of *something* you do better than average. *Everyone* has innate gifts and talents. Some are just more obvious than others.

At some point, everyone helps another person. Have you ever had some comforting words for a friend or family member or written a poem and shared it with someone? Are you an athlete who played team sports? Do you have a job where you work with other people or provide services to others? I'm sure you can think of countless times when you helped someone, whether it was in a big way or in a small way.

Sharing your gifts is not necessarily a ginormous feat where you're single-handedly saving humanity! It can be simple and subtle. You may be a natural counselor, but never viewed yourself as one. You could be a healer, but think that's something only in science fiction movies. You might be a teacher, but think they're only in schools. These lines of thinking make gift-sharing seem out of reach for many.

Teaching, counseling, and healing are humanity's foremost spiritual gifts. A spiritual gift is an ability or skill that you have that can help someone else, usually in a spiritual or non-secular way. We all have one of these spiritual gifts inside of us. It doesn't matter if you are religious or if you live a "spiritual life," you still possess the capacity to heal, counsel, and/or teach.

A healer is someone who lessens another living being's suffering. Teachers share information or things that will help people. And counselors help people deal with life's issues, challenges, and obstacles.

There are many faiths that teach that our purpose is to help each other. By sharing who you are with your friends, family or others, you help the world. The *world* is simply other people. Whether you help 2 people or 2 *billion* isn't important. What's important is that you're sharing your gift.

Many people feel like they only share their skills at work or that a job is the only place one can make a difference. This is limited thinking. No matter what skills you have, there are plenty of outlets for them to be shared. Sharing can occur among family and friends, your local community or even globally via the internet. Don't limit yourself to sharing your gift in any one setting! Step back and look at the whole picture. You will see that there are endless ways to share your gifts and talents with the world.

Whatever skills, talents and gifts you have, be certain to share them with others. Take the time to determine the best ways for you to help someone else. This will be one of the best gifts you ever give, and the Universe will always return your efforts in beautifully miraculous ways.

Learning Life Lessons

The last of the three universal purposes is learning life lessons. This one may be the most challenging of all. Most lessons are difficult. That's why they are called lessons. Many times, we avoid tough lessons because they cause us to feel uncomfortable. At times, they can even cause us pain.

In school, some lessons are harder to learn than others. You master certain classes and assignments, but there is usually always one class or lesson that challenged you. Regardless of your level of intelligence or your grade point average, there were still lessons that were harder than others to learn.

The lessons we are taught in school are analogous to the lessons we learn on Earth. For instance, you may be a talented singer, but have major stage fright. How are you going to perform and share your gift when you're deathly afraid of doing it in front of other people? Is stage fright a lesson? Sort of. But the *greater* lesson is in the REASON why you have it in the first place.

We tend to judge things on the surface level as humans. Stage fright could stem from insecurities or issues with confidence. It could also be related to competitive tension or the singer's own perfectionism. The end result is not always in the lesson itself. Lessons can appear in one area of your life or in some cases, they can show up in many areas of your life. It all depends on what lessons you decided you wanted to learn during your present incarnation.

If your gifts are something you readily share with others, then what can prevent you from being able to share those gifts are your life lessons. Think of things that you KNOW you should change or overcome. Not what other people think. What *YOU* think. Nobody has to tell you your true life lessons. They nag at you all the time, constantly presenting themselves as recurring or looped thoughts leading to feeling a lack of progression in life. These looped thoughts are like broken records in the mind. They frequently remind you of what you *know* you must work to overcome and master.

Successfully learning our life lessons lead to our growth and evolution. The more you share your gifts, the more your soul will evolve. Many of the lessons you must learn are directly related to the gifts you have to share.

146

Learn, grow, and share. Do not deprive yourself and the rest of the world of the benefits of your universal purposes.

LIFE GUIDANCE

What comes to mind when you hear the words, *life purpose*? Take a minute or two to think about this question *(insert 5 minute pause with dramatic background music)*. The words, *life purpose*, can sound a little overwhelming. After all, your life encompasses an extended period of time which makes this accomplishment seem too huge and maybe even *impossible* to achieve. Doesn't it? Or does *life purpose* sound like violins playing in the background as chakra-colored unicorns gallop around? Yeah, kinda corny, but I'm trying to make a point.

Truth is we put way too much energy into concepts and ideas. Ask anyone who is living a life full of purpose and they will tell you that it's simple and enjoyable. Most people's lives are complex and problematic because they are going against the flow. Learning to follow your guidance will aid you in simplifying your life and living with more purpose.

All throughout your life, you've been "guided." In this chapter, you will learn about the spiritual guidance that's always directing you. This guidance mainly shows itself in three forms: signs, synchronicity, and intuition. Trusting that you are being guided is a reassuring feeling. Once you learn how this guidance manifests, allow yourself to recognize these patterns as they show up in your life.

Signs

Signs are just as they sound. A sign lets you know where you are or where you're headed. You can be listening to music and the next song that plays is your deceased grandmother's favorite song. Many see this as a sign that she is near or saying, "Hi." *Or* you can be riding in your car when you see a billboard which reads, "Be all you can achieve," and you take that as a literal message or sign.

We all know what signs are because we've all experienced them. Some signs are neither visual nor audible. Have you ever walked into a room and got an uneasy feeling in your gut? Did you take that as a sign of possible danger or chaos? Yup, betcha did.

Now, let's say you had a disturbing dream the night before you entered the room and got an uneasy feeling. In your dream, you were faced with some major mishaps when you walked into a particular room. You wake up and realize it was a dream, but it felt so *real*.

Next, you get out of bed and turn the radio on. You happen to tune in just as your favorite radio personality is in the middle of describing a dream they had about getting beaten in a blue colored room. Coincidence? Let's keep going.

Remember, in this scenario, the dream actually leads you into going somewhere and entering a room where you immediately get a gut feeling of discomfort or danger.

Now, keep in mind that the occurrence of two or more signs revealed within a short period of time is called *synchronicity* which we'll cover next.

A sign can be *anything* that catches your attention. Signs usually elicit a feeling of being given direction or a significant message. Learning to read signs will help you be more purposeful. They are always guiding you if you remain attentive and aware.

Here are some examples of signs in everyday life:

•   You're at the grocery store and someone drops a loaf of bread in front of you.
        You then remember that you're out of bread at the house. The loaf of bread was a sign.
•   You wake up thinking about what you should be doing with your life. After you brush your teeth, you get on Facebook to scroll for a bit. The first post you see is someone talking about something they're doing and it resonates with you. Their post was a sign.
•   While watching a YouTube video, the advertisement at the beginning is about weight loss and dieting. It may resonate with you because you know you should adopt a healthier lifestyle. The ad was a sign.
•   You're at the gym working out when you notice that there is too much weight on the bench. You get a feeling that you can lift it even though it's above your max. The weights become a sign.
•   While reading a passage in a book, you come across a character with your last name. He or she introduces themselves along with their occupation. The

150

occupation resonates with you as something you could see yourself doing. The character's occupation is a sign.

Signs will stick out to you. The key is to not look for them. Just be open to receive them as they come. Focus on being receptive more than searching and analyzing. Your signs may be big or small, mundane or highly purposeful. In my experience, the signs seem to guide me to exactly where I need to go, and I *love* to travel, so I'm always up for the trip!

Synchronicity

A synchronicity is a meaningful coincidence. It is two or more related things, circumstances or events that occur at unexpected times in unexpected places. Synchronicity is like a sign on steroids. Because a synchronicity is made up of two or more signs, it has double or even *triple* the amount of power. This form of guidance is very important when it shows up in your life.

In our example of danger in the previous section, the person experienced the same theme in three different manners, in a dream, on the radio and in waking life. The three coincidental events make a synchronicity. Synchronicities send a signal to us that something significant is occurring and provide invaluable guidance.

Guidance is a form of events getting our attention. Call it God or the Creator, the Universe or the Cosmos, for whatever reason, "*It*" uses various ways to guide us. There's probably no better way of getting our attention than to throw two or more signs at us. By the third one, I'm sure you'll start to take notice.

Synchronicity appears in life when you really need to pay attention to the guidance being provided. For me, it seems as if multiple coincidences popped up on my path in crucial moments. Looking back, it was the synchronicities that helped me discover my highest calling, which is to teach.

So, to reiterate, two or more signs or coincidences are called a synchronicity. The more coincidences and related signs you receive, the greater the synchronicity. Look at it as Spirit working hard to get you a message if you're getting multiple signs.

Here are some examples of synchronicity in everyday life:

• You go to your friend's house and they have a book about dreams on the table. You then go to the grocery store and notice a woman in the checkout line wearing a shirt that reads, "Dreams are what you make them." You get home and your neighbor tells you they had a crazy dream last night. Three signs or coincidences about dreams make a synchronicity.

• The first post you see on Facebook sticks out to you. Your friend shared a story about someone traveling to Spain. You've always wanted to go to Spain. A few minutes later, another friend messages you letting you know that they're going to Madrid in a few weeks. Your synchronicity involves going to Spain.

• You start a new job at a prestigious company, but you really don't want to work for someone else. The first day there, you befriend someone who is about to quit so that they can start their own business. During orientation, your trainer tells the new hires that he used to own his own company. This synchronicity is associated with owning a business.

Make sure to pay attention and follow your synchronicities. Any sign you see more than once in a short period of time will lead you to greater purpose. Learn to recognize and trust this guidance.

Intuition

Intuition, or simply knowing without rational or logical reasoning, is experienced as having an internal knowing or thought devoid of external stimuli. It is the acquisition of information without rational thinking. Intuitive thoughts are universal phenomena that everyone experiences on a continuous basis.

Have you ever had an idea just "pop" into your head? Ever thought of doing something different even when you were not focused on doing anything? Have you received insights into someone in your life even when they weren't around? If you answered, "Yes," to any of these questions, then you've had an intuitive thought.

Intuition is a vital guiding system that many people often dismiss or overlook. In addition to signs and synchronicity, intuition gives us another voice of reason, another source of direction. Your life has great purpose and the Universe constantly uses these three forms of communication to guide you.

Despite intuition being mentioned last, it's probably the most common form of guidance. This is because our thoughts are constant. Intertwined with our regular thoughts are intuitive downloads. The key is to notice thoughts that are off-beat or unrelated to your current thought process. The thoughts that seem out of place are usually intuitive. They tend to pop into our minds when we are not thinking too hard. When these unrelated thoughts pop in, pay more attention to them because they have meaning. Usually, this meaning makes more sense in hindsight.

Have you ever done something or befriended someone but had an ill feeling prior only to find out later that your feelings were correct? What you experienced was an intuitive thought letting you know something was awry even though you had no evidence to validate your reasoning. This is how intuition works. It's the voice of reason that comes to you when you're least expecting it.

Early on my path, I kept a journal with all my intuitive downloads. I did this for about a year. When I went back to read my entries, it was obvious that I was being guided and nudged in specific directions. That journal became a map showing me where I was traveling. That's the power in paying attention to your intuition.

The best way to increase intuition is through meditation. Meditation has become very popular and mainstream over the years. This is because it's almost a necessity to increase intuitive thoughts. Also, intuitive thoughts are the source of creativity. To create something means to do something that has never been done before or to do something in an innovative manner. Because you're working to accomplish something new, you need new thoughts to do it. These new thoughts can be seen as intuition.

Your intuitive thoughts are filled with many new ideas. From success in business to personal development to any other area of life you can think of, you can receive intuitive thoughts, or ideas that come to you for a specific purpose. Many great inventions and businesses were created based on intuition. Art, music, poetry, dance, and methods for self-improvement, all were created from intuition.

Here are some examples of how intuition manifests in everyday life:

• You're on the phone with a friend, when all of a sudden you get a thought about your child getting hurt. This thought is unrelated to your conversation. The thought about your child getting hurt is intuitive.
• You're out jogging when you receive an idea to create an app that helps people find lost loved ones. Obviously the thought had nothing to do with jogging or even health. The idea is an intuitive thought.

- You get a random idea on how to improve something. That idea was intuitive.
- While washing dishes, you get a thought to go to your boss for a raise. That thought was intuitive because it had nothing to do with washing dishes.

Life guidance is an invaluable resource provided to us by the Universe to assist us with moving in the direction in which our soul desires to go. Intuition is the most common form of guidance we receive, and when that's not enough, it's usually followed by a sign or two. If we *still* don't get the message, these signs will multiply into a series of coincidences, or synchronicities.

I highly recommend that you keep a journal to record your spiritual life guidance. Miracles happen when you train yourself to notice spiritual guidance. The spiritual guidance that will lead you to greater purpose comes in the form of signs, synchronicity, and intuition. A journal will let both you and the Universe know that this guidance is important to you. It's essential to know that with whatever you deem important, the Universe will agree and comply by delivering more of it to you. In other words, ultimately, you will receive more of what you think is important once you begin to take notice of your life guidance. Training yourself to make entries in your spiritual life guidance journal will emphatically relay to the Universe that you see the signs, synchronicity and intuition you are receiving as something helpful.

Making purposeful choices and recognizing your guidance is a fundamental template for living life.

Imagine knowing a way out for every obstacle in life. Could you imagine knowing your next moves and where those moves will take you? Imagine a life where there is little confusion on what you should be doing and how. You have a chance to realize it by focusing on what's in your heart and keeping a journal of your guidance.

Please Note: This book will not serve you unless you put what you've learned from it into action. Period. No exceptions. I did not write *Now Purpose Manual* just to add more information to your mental database. My goal is help you attain a purposeful life and these gems, if properly put into action, will do just that and *so* much more!

I know you would not have taken the time to read this book if there wasn't something inside you that wanted to grow, to change for the better. This book has given you the tools. Start with the Light that you want to make more purposeful. Complete a task or action that pushes the needle forward. You've spun your wheels long enough. I know you're ready to drive! I *know* you want to live your purpose now!

So, for the last time…

When is your purpose?

COMMON QUESTIONS

Now that you've finished reading *Now Purpose Manual*, I thought I'd address some commonly asked questions with regard to using the tools to discover your *Now Purpose*. I hope the information here offers additional support and assists you with experiencing greater success in your quest to live a more purposeful life.

I read the entire book and I still don't know what I should be doing right now?

Answer: Go back to the "Lights of Awareness" chapter or section within the area of life chapter that you've selected and just ask yourself the questions. What do you want to do more? What do you want to do less? What do you want to stop doing? What do want to start? Then choose the one that pulls at your heart the *most*.

What's the difference between life's purpose and life's calling?

Answer: I feel like they're the same thing. However, both seem like something that is far away or unachievable. This is why I use the words 'Now Purpose.' So, no matter how you look at it, you still want to focus on *today*.

How do I know if I'm on the right track?

Answer: I honestly think this is one of the most crippling questions you can have on your path. This is because you are *always* where you're supposed to be, so you *must* be on the right track. Now, if you don't like where you are on your journey, then it's up to *you* to make a change. *Now Purpose Manual* will help you to identify and make the changes necessary for living a life that's more fulfilling and *definitely* more purposeful.

Are there any other systems that will help me find out more about myself and my purpose?

Answer: Yes. The best systems to gain greater self-awareness and guidance are Astrology and Numerology. Astrology is more detailed, but it's also more complex. Numerology is simple and will provide quick answers. Do you research and decide which you'd prefer to explore.

How can I use this book to find a major for college?

Answer: Refer to the *Now Purpose in Business* chapter. Whatever focus you are drawn to, let that be your major. For example, if you have Lights and awareness answers that identify a specific subject like mathematics, then choose a major that is math based. Unfortunately, you may change your mind while in college. Just make sure you are willing to be flexible if you're not completely sure.

Can I *really* start living my purpose today?

Answer: Yes! As mentioned throughout the book, your purpose will change as you grow and evolve. When you were old enough to drive, your purpose was to get a valid driver's license. After you got your license, your purpose may have changed to getting a car or permission from your parents to drive theirs. Likewise, once you had access to the car, your purpose probably changed again as you had various destinations and goals you wished to reach involving the use of the car. Your purpose will change in most areas of life as you progress.

My Lights of Awareness seem small and not too purposeful. Am I doing it right?

Answer: As mentioned above and throughout the book, your purpose will change as you grow and evolve. Big purposes usually stay a dream or a wish. In order to achieve bigger purposes or goals you must chip away at them with small actionable steps. Your Lights are probably those small actionable steps. Focus on them. *That's* your starting point.

I feel like I'm living a life of purpose. Do I need to read this book?

Answer: If you feel like it will be helpful, why not? *Now Purpose Manual* was written for those who are having a hard time finding purpose in their lives. If you're living with purpose, then you've already met the objective of this book. However, even if you are living a purposeful life, it is likely that you still have evolving goals within your purpose. It can be beneficial to use the tools in this book to nudge you even farther into your purpose. Look at your longer term goals and ask yourself the, "How," and "Why," questions. Applying the tools to an already purposeful life can make your experience on Earth even more powerful.

Can someone help me find my Now Purpose?

Answer: There are many counselors and guides in the world that offer life guidance. I have helped many souls over the years find more meaning in life and their spiritual practice. If you want to take things a step farther with one-on-one support, you can schedule a consultation with me through my website: SAliMyers.com

Can I get paid for living my purpose?

Answer: I believe that most people have a gift or talent that they can use to help other people. Typically, you are compensated for helping others. A waiter at a restaurant gets paid to serve food. The waiter's purpose is to provide food and drinks to the customer. They are tipped and receive a paycheck. Are they paid for their purpose? Absolutely! If you feel like your purpose involves compensation, then you must place yourself in the best position to receive. This includes working somewhere, starting a business around your purpose, or running some sort of project that allows you to share your gifts.

I'm in the golden years of life. Am I too old to have a purpose?

Answer: Absolutely not! You are still on earth for a reason. Your *Now Purpose* may not be in the areas of business, personal development or finance, but, you may want to make your relationships and family more purposeful. Regardless of your age, I'm sure there's *something* that you are drawn to. *That's* your purpose today!

How do I know if something is right or wrong for my purpose or path?

Answer: You *won't* know until you "walk" it. I can't stress enough that your heart is the best judge on your path. If something pops into your Lights of Awareness, it's there for a reason. How can you discover that reason? Through your experiences. How do you know *anything* without experience? Experience allows us to know what is "right" or "wrong" for us. Obviously, there are *some* things we don't need to experience to determine this, but I'm sure you'd identify those with your Yellow or Black Lights.

What if I know my purpose but don't know how to do it?

Answer: I'm sure there is something you *CAN* do. If you have completed your Lights of Awareness, then you should have some actionable steps to help you get closer to your goal. If you have no steps, then you didn't make

162

an adequately significant effort. Try again. You may have to start by doing something you don't want to do in order to get to where you want to go.

I am having a hard time coming up with Lights of Awareness. Why?

Answer: What you truly want probably seems too far away. This only means that you have many steps before you get there, but that's okay. Force yourself to break your goal up into bite-sized pieces, or small actionable steps. If you still need help, consider consulting with a professional like me or someone who has been successful with what you're aiming to achieve.

I want to find purpose in every area of life. Can I *do* that?

Answer: Yes, you can do whatever you want! It may not be easy, but it's totally possible. Just remember, beginning with one or two areas of life is what is recommended. If you want to focus on every area of life right now, that means you see lack in every aspect of your life. It isn't very realistic to think that you can instantly fix everything you see wrong with yourself.

Now Purpose Manual was written to help you find meaning in your life *today*. I doubt that your spirit is guiding you to overhaul your entire life all at once. I'm sure you feel called to one or two areas of life that mean something to you right now. I'd start there.

How can you tell the difference between your purpose and talent(s)?

Answer: Great question! Unfortunately, same answer. Your heart and current situation will tell you. Let me give you an example:

I love to spit bars! The first time I went into a real studio to record original songs, I was *geeked!* That was probably over 20 years ago. My friends back then used to tell me how ill I was (in a good way). I was definitely one of the best rappers in the clique. My point is I had talent in rap, yet I never felt the need to pursue a career in it. It never called me or motivated me to let people hear me.

Some talents may not need to be used for a major part of your purpose. But just like my amateur rap career, I plan on using my rapping abilities to deliver spiritual content in the future. In a way, I'm still using my talent but it's not a focal point of my purpose. Only you can decide if your talent directly relates to your purpose. Listen to your heart.

I'm unhappy in my career, but think it's my calling. Can this be true?

Answer: Your calling or *Now Purpose* may involve *real* work. The difference between working on something purposeful compared to just working is the level of fulfillment that you experience. Purposeful work is very

164

gratifying when you're done. It's not always enjoyable in the process, but the payoff seems worth the effort.

If you are unhappy in your career, but think it's your calling, simply ask yourself if you are gaining or *losing* energy. If you feel drained, it's probably not your calling or right environment. If energized, you may just be in a slump.

What if I feel stuck?

Answer: Get unstuck! Joking. Well…not really. To get unstuck, you must *move*. Action is how we get out of binds and strongholds. Just start doing something, especially one of your Green or Black Lights.

Made in the USA
Columbia, SC
02 September 2020